ON GRACE AND FREE CHOICE

ON GRACE
& FREE CHOICE

De gratia et libero arbitrio

BY
BERNARD OF CLAIRVAUX

Translated by Daniel O'Donovan OCSO
Introduction by Bernard McGinn

Cistercian Publications Inc.
Kalamazoo, Michigan
Spencer, Massachusetts

1988

This translation has been made from the critical Latin edition prepared by Jean Leclercq OSB and H.M. Rochais under the sponsorship of the Order of Cistercians and published by Editiones Cistercienses, Piazza Tempio di Diana, 14, Rome.

This translation appeared previously in *Bernard of Clairvaux: Treatises III* (1977).

Available in Britain and Europe from
A.R. Mowbray & Co Ltd
St Thomas House   Becket Street
Oxford OX1 1SJ

Available elsewhere (including Canada) from
Cistercian Publications / Distribution
St Joseph's Abbey
Spencer, MA 01562

Printed in the United States of America

TABLE OF CONTENTS

ON GRACE AND FREE CHOICE

INTRODUCTION

WHILE ST BERNARD'S FAME rests primarily upon his reputation as a mystical theologian, as illustrated especially in his *Sermons on the Song of Songs*, it is safe to say that this mystical theory cannot be understood apart from its dogmatic base. Hence the treatise entitled *Grace and Free Choice*, the most profound and influential of the Abbot of Clairvaux's dogmatic works, even in an *a priori* sense occupies a central place in his corpus. Given this importance, it is lamentable that so little attention has been devoted to the treatise-some remarks in E. Gilson's *The Mystical Theology of St. Bernard*,[1] a monograph in Italian by G. Venuta,[2] the thesis of M. Standaert on Bernard's doctrine of the image of God,[3] and a handful of articles are all that the extensive Bernard literature has to show.[4] One previous translation of the treatise into English

1. First published in 1934. English translation by A. H. C. Downes (N.Y., 1940), especially chapter 2.
2. *Libero Arbitrio e Libertà della Grazia nel Pensiero di San Bernardo* (Rome, 1953).
3. *La doctrine de l'image chez Saint Bernard* (Louvain, 1947), *In Sylloge Excerptorum e Dissertationibus*, Vol. 14, fasc. 4. Also published in *Ephemerides Theologicae Lovaniensis*, 23 (1947): 70-129 (this pagination will be followed here).
4. O. Schaffner, "Die 'nobilis Deo creatura' des heiligen Bernhard von Clairvaux," *Geist und Leben*, 23 (1950): 43-57; L. Sartori, "Natura e Grazia nella Dottrina de San Bernardo," *Studia Patavina*, 1 (1954): 41-64; A. Forest, "Das Erlebnis des Consensus Voluntatis beim heiligen Bernhard," *Bernhard von Clairvaux, Mönch und Mystiker* (Wiesbaden, 1955): 120-27; E. Kleinedam, "*De triplici libertate*. Anselm von Laon oder Bernhard von Clairvaux? " *Cîteaux*, 11 (1960): 56-62; G. Bavaud, "Les rapports de la grâce et du libre arbitre. Un dialogue entre saint Bernard, saint Thomas d'Aquin et Calvin," *Verbum Caro*, 14 (1960): 328-38; and U. Faust, "Bernhards 'Liber de Gratia et Libero Arbitrio': Bedeutung, Quellen und Einfluss", *Analecta Monastica* 6 (*Studia Anselmiana* 50, Rome, 1962).

exists.[5] No excuse then need be made for a new attempt to assay the significance of the treatise, whatever the judgments to be made regarding the performance. This "Introduction" will not only attempt to isolate the major themes of the treatise but will also strive to present a determination of its place in the deveoopment of the discussion of grace and free will, one of the fundamental question of the history of Christian thought.

THE GENRE OF THE TREATISE

No great difficulties of dating or of textual transmission are presented by the treatise on *Grace and Free Choice*. The work is an early product of Bernard's pen, probably written about the year 1128,[6] and thus a companion piece to such other early treatises as the *Apologia* to William of St Thierry, *The Steps of Humility,* and *On Loving of God.* The recent edition of J. Leclercq and H. Rochais has established a definitive text,[7] the basis for the present translation, and also afforded a discussion of the textual transmission.[8] More important for understanding the work is the determination of the literary genre to which it belongs.

Anselm Le Bail has noted that the mystical theology of the great Cistercian authors presupposes a theory of the soul and its powers. Many Cistercians have left us works explicitly devoted to the soul, Bernard has not. Le Bail and others would see in the *Grace and Free Choice* the equivalent of such a treatise.[9] While the work is among the most important documents for the understanding of the Abbot's theory of

5. W. W. Williams, *The Treatise of St. Bernard Concerning Grace and Free Will* (London, 1920).

6. See J. J Leclercq and H. M. Rochais, *Sancti Bernardi Opera,* 9 vols (Rome, 1955-) (Hereafter cited as OB) 3:157.

7. OB 3:165-203.

8. OB 3:157-63.

9. "Saint Bernard," *Dictionnaire de Spiritualité,* Vol. 1, cc. 1461; 1472 (Paris, 1935). See also Schaffner, "Die 'nobilis Deo'" 45; and Venuta, *Libero Arbitrio,* 17, note 1, who notes the qualifications with which this description must be taken.

the soul, and of man in general,[10] neither in form nor in content is it best understood as a *De anima* treatise. Another hint at the genre of the work may bring us nearer the truth. In his discussion of three "blocs" at the basis of Bernard's mysticism, E. Gilson admitted a certain incompleteness in his analysis. "For there is at least a fourth 'bloc' that entered into his patiently constructed edifice. This is the doctrine of liberty contained in the Epistle to the Romans, whence Bernard drew his *De gratia et libero arbitrio*."[11] The Abbot himself asserts the extent of his dependence on Paul toward the end of the treatise when he proudly claims: "We trust the reader may be pleased to find that we have never strayed far from the Apostle's meaning."[12] While making use of a wide range of Paul's other writings, especially the Epistles to the Corinthians and to the Galatians, it is certainly the Epistle to the Romans which is the major Scriptural basis for the *Grace and Free Choice.*[13]

In one sense, then, the treatise might be said to be Bernard's commentary on Romans. And yet even this does not fully capture its essence. *Grace and Free Choice* is not constructed in the form of a scriptural commentary, either of the traditional patristic-monastic type or of the Scholastic variety then in its infancy. Rather than being controlled by the order of the sacred text itself, the Abbot of Clairvaux fastens his attention on the essential problems of the relation of grace and freedom posed by Romans. The order is his own. Augustine's treatises against the Pelagians and Semi-Pelagians provide the nearest models for the work, and Augustine also gives us a succinct description of its character and aim: "For in this letter of mine [*The Spirit and the Letter*] we have not

---

10. For Bernard's anthropology see W. Hiss, *Die Anthropologie Bernhards von Clairvaux* (Berlin, 1964); and E. von Ivánka, "La structure de l'âme selon Saint Bernard," *Saint Bernard Théologien*, ASOC 9 (1953): 202-08.

11. Gilson, 220, note 23.

12. Gra 14:48.

13. Bernard cites it eighteen times explicitly and twenty-five times implicitly. It should be noted how seldom the abbot engages in allegorical interpretation in a dogmatic treatise of this nature.

undertaken to expound this epistle, but only, mainly on its authority, to demonstrate, so far as we are able, that we are assisted by divine aid toward the achievement of righteousness. . . ."[14]

The key to understanding this central work of Bernard's is to be found in its place in the history of the theological problem of grace and free will. What were the issues involved? What solutions had already been offered and which were influential upon the Abbot? What was the nature of his contribution and what further history was it to have? An adequate answer to all these questions would surely involve the equivalent of a history of Christian theology. Our primary task, of course, is the analysis of the work itself, but this analysis demands some sketch of the background out of which the Abbot wrote.

The problems of the nature of the human will and its relation to freedom are not ones that are peculiar to the history of Christianity. Many of the most important issues involved were already familiar to pagan philosophical traditions.[15] Nevertheless, it cannot be denied that the fundamental tenets of the Christian faith placed the problem of freedom in a central position, and did so by introducing a new series of complications and paradoxes into an already involved area.

As a means of providing some insight into the patristic and medieval evolution of the question, Christian speculation concerning human freedom may be viewed as influenced throughout its history by two complexes of related, but still distinguishable, concerns. The first could be termed the abstract complex, that which deals with the reconciliation of divine foreknowledge and predestination with the contin-

---

14. *De spiritu et littera* 12:20 (*CSEL* 60:173). Translation from *Nicene and Post-Nicene Fathers*. Series 1, Vol. 5, 91.

15. Two general surveys are V. Bourke, *Will in Western Thought* (N.Y., 1964); and M. Adler, *The Idea of Freedom* (N.Y., 1958-61), 2 Vols. Important for the medieval context is the chapter "Free-Will and Christian Liberty," in E. Gilson, *The Spirit of Mediaeval Philosophy* (N.Y., 1940).

gency of human actions. It explores the implications inherent
in the dilemma: either God truly foreknows and infallibly
causes all things and hence everything happens necessarily, or
at least some human actions happen contingently as the prod-
ucts of free choice and therefore God's knowledge and will
are limited. The second complex is concrete and historical,
concerned with the relation of man's freedom of choice in
the various states of history to sin and to grace. More particularly, granted the fallen state of man, what freedom, if any,
does he still retain to choose good or evil? What kind of
freedom did Adam have before the Fall? And finally, if justification is entirely the work of God's grace, what kind of
freedom remains to the Christian in the state of grace? As
Bernard's interlocutor put it in the exchange reported at the
beginning of the treatise: "What part do *you* play, then, . . .
or what reward or prize do you hope for, if it is all God's
work?"[16]
Obsiously, the two sets of concerns influenced each other
and were frequently considered together in the course of the
same treatises; nevertheless, the history of Western theology
shows the usefulness of distinguishing the two. The abstract
complex of "providence-predestination-contingency" can be
thought of as the more general one upon which the solutions
worked out in the complex "sin-grace-freedom." This view,
however, presupposes a somewhat speculative notion of theology and a positive attitude to the relation between philosophical and Christian speculation which was on some occasions not present and on others either deliberately rejected or
considered unessential. Yet the abstract complex should not
be thought of as purely philosophical, no matter how much
the complexities of its treatment owe to philosophical sys-
tems, particularly that of Aristotle. The Scriptures do speak
of providence and predestination as well as of sin and grace,
and thus virtually every Christian theology has had to take
some stand with regard to certain of the problems involved in
what we have called the abstract complex, even if it refuses

16. Gra 1:1.

to consider them in the light of philogophical categories. In short, while our two complexes may very well be thought of after the manner of ideal-types, they have a real heuristic value in helping us to structure the history of Christian speculation on freedom.

The dominance of the concrete schema of sin-grace-freedom during the patristic and early medieval period, as well as a particular cast which it took, is indicated by the very title of Bernard's treatise *De gratia et libero arbitrio, On Grace and Free Choice.* It is important to note that it is the term "free choice" (*liberum arbitrium*) and not "free will" (*libera voluntas*) which is the operative one in Bernard and throughout most of the period in question. The problem was essentially that of man's ability to perform free acts. An explanation of freedom need not be intimately involved with a developed theory of the will; particularly before the period of High Scholasticism medieval authors rarely took up their pens to write treatises *De voluntate.*

One great advantage of the term *liberum arbitrium* was its inclusion of the rational component in freedom. Despite the stress on lack of coercion as the essence of freedom, patristic and medieval authors were never unaware of the delicate problems involved in relating the action of the intellect and the will. Certain High Scholastic writers tried to solve these problems by holding that *liberum arbitrium* was a separate faculty in man, superior to intellect and will.[17] Even in Thomas Aquinas it was not until the *Prima Secundae* of the *Summa* (1269) that the term *liberum arbitrium* lost equal footing with *voluntas* in the systematic analysis of human freedom.[18] Thus it is around the fundamental problems involved in the term *liberum arbitrium* rather than around the systematic concern to elucidate the notion of will that the patristic and medieval approach to the problem developed.

17. For example, Peter of Capua, Geoffrey of Poitiers, and Albert the Great. In this connection see O. Lottin, "Libre arbitre et liberté depuis Saint Anselme jusqu'a la fin du XIIIe siècle," in *Psychologie et morale aux XIIe et XIIIe siècles,* 6 Vols. (Louvain-Gembloux, 1942-1960), 1: 219-20.

18. See B. J Lonergan, *Grace and Freedom: Operative Grace in the Thought of Thomas Aquinas* (London-N.Y., 1971), 93.

The theology of Augustine of Hippo provides the *terminus a quo* for the treatment of grace and free choice in the medieval period. Naturally, it is impossible to give any idea of the complex evolution and profundity of his ideas in a brief compass; but in terms of the ideal complexes we have delineated, some broad characterization of his central concerns and influence on the medieval context may be made. First of all, it should be noted that Augustine's attention was largely restricted to the concrete complex of "sin-grace-freedom," partly due to the exigencies of polemic and partly to the philosophical and theological horizon within which he worked. Secondly, Augustine equated the will with the exercise of free choice[19] and provided much impetus for that tradition which discussed grace and freedom primarily under the rubric of *liberum arbitrium* rather than *voluntas*. Finally, he was much concerned, especially in the later stages of his career, with problems of providence and predestination; but in only a few texts was this concern developed within the abstract context of contingency and necessity.[20]

Augustine's views on grace and freedom are polemical, dogmatic, normative, and unfinished. They are polemical insofar as their origin is to be sought not so much in developments out of his own theoretical concerns (e.g., the *De Trinitate*) as in responses he was called upon to make to the challenge of Pelagianism.[21] They are dogmatic in that his primary intent was not so much to seek to understand (insofar as human capability can) the mystery of the divine will and human freedom, but to display the faith of the Church as based upon the Scriptures.[22] Despite the unsystematic and partial

19. Bourke, *Will in Western Thought,* 81-2; and E. Gilson, *The Christian Philosophy of St. Augustine* (N.Y., 1967), 157.

20. In the *De civitate Dei* 5:9-10; and the *De libero arbitrio* 3:2-4, Augustine treats the relation between foreknowledge and contingency by introducing the distinction between the kinds of necessity which was to become one of the touchstones of the abstract complex.

21. For a recent survey in English of Augustine's theological response to Pelagianism and Semi-Pelagianism see E. Teselle, *Augustine the Theologian* (N.Y., 1970), Chap. 5:2; and 6:1-2.

22. On the dogmatic character of Augustine's theology of grace, see Lonergan, *Grace and Freedom,* 4-5.

character of his writings, however, their magnitude, insight, and power were to assure them a normative position in the history of Western theology. A medieval theologian might venture to reinterpret Augustine; he would rarely openly disagree with him. Finally, Augustine's thought on grace and freedom was unfinished—at least in the sense that its unsystematic character and polemical cast could easily lead to demands for the harmonization of divergent expressions and inconsistencies, real or imagined. His work was also incomplete in the sense that the speculative thrusts made into the knottiest problems of grace and free choice, to some minds at least, could only be solved by an advance across the board to a new and more systematic level in the treatment of grace and its related problems.

Insofar as the influence of the content of Augustine's views on the medieval development is concerned, several general tenets are of special significance for the path that we will trace.[23] In his writings against the Pelagians and Semi-Pelagians the bishop of Hippo, faithful to his mentor St Paul, made it quite clear that the total initiative in the life of grace rested with God and not with man. So despite the loss of the canons of the Second Synod of Orange (529) during the medieval period,[24] a perspicacious reading of Augustine could always forestall an overly optimistic view of the freedom of fallen man to perform any saving action. But Augustine by no means concluded from this that fallen man had completely lost the capacity of freedom of choice, nor did he assert that some kind of assent was not necessary in the process of justification. Granted the great difficulties of reconciling freedom of choice with the inability to choose the saving good, absolute determinism remained abhorrent to the

23. The literature is vast. Along with the general works already mentioned, H. McSorley in *Luther: Right or Wrong?* (N.Y., 1969), 63-110, contains an analysis of Augustine's major treatises on these questions.

24. See H. Bouillard, *Conversion et grâce chez S. Thomas d'Aquin* (Paris, 1944), 98-102; 114-21.

African Doctor.[25] Furthermore, his attempt of an historical survey of the state of free choice in the various periods of salvation history was to be a topic of major concern throughout the history of Western theology.

If Augustine is the master of the concrete complex of "sin-grace-freedom," then Boethius may be taken as the major influence in the less immediately significant, but eventually very important, abstract schema of "providence-predestination-contingency." His long discussion of the relation of divine foreknowledge and the possibility of free choice in the *Consolation of Philosophy*[26] not only laid stress upon distinguishing varieties of necessity as Augustine had done, but also stressed the presentiality of God's knowledge as a key to overcoming the false implications involved in the notion of foreknowledge.[27] In his second commentary on Aristotle's *On Interpretation*, Boethius advanced a definition of free choice which served to transmit the Peripatetic intellectual emphasis to medieval authors.[28]

Thus the early twelfth-century context within which Bernard wrote his treatise was open to influences from both the abstract as well as the concrete complex, though the concrete question of the historical states of freedom predominated. We must not think that Early Scholastic speculation on grace and free choice was nothing more than a repetition of Augustine or a series of footnotes to his treatises. Still, it is true to say that the theology of grace and freedom of the time was, in large measure, the first attempts to come to grips with the speculative problems implicit in the dogmatic heritage of the Augustinian tradition. Such an immense task could scarcely

---

25. McSorley, *Luther,* 109-10. The distinction between the freedom left to man after the fall and the freedom to choose the good is frequently expressed by the difference between *liberum arbitrium* and *libertas.*

26. Book 4, prosa 6 to the end of Book 5 (Loeb Classical Library, ed. E. Rand, 338-410).

27. Book 5, prosa 6 (ed. 398-410).

28. "Liberum de voluntate iudicium." *In librum Aristotelis de interpretatione libri sex. Editio secunda,* 3 (PL 64:492-3). On the importance of this definition see Lottin, *Psychologie et Morale,* 16-7, note 3; and Gilson, *The Spirit of Mediaeval Philosophy,* 310-1.

have been initiated with other than halting steps; the fundamental lines of its development were not to be clarified until well into the thirteenth century. The careful research of Artur Landgraf and Odo Lottin among others, as well as the insights of Bernard Lonergan provide some avenue into this complex world.[29]

Among the issues of fundamental speculative significance with which Early Scholastic theology was concerned we may isolate the definition of free choice (*liberum arbitrium*),[30] the determination of the various states of liberty, and the nature of the. causal relationship between grace and free choice as central. While it may be true that the adequate correlation of these questions was eventually achieved only by the emergence of the notion of the supernatural habit in the thirteenth century,[31] the intellectual energy which twelfth-century authors put into the investigation of these questions is evidence of the speculative exigence at work in this early period. These men were by no means content merely to repeat the wisdom of their forefathers. Rather they sought to achieve a balance between traditional theological authority and the more systematic demands of their contemporaries. The variety and invention with which they approached this task is what gives the early twelfth century its distinctive flavor.

It is scarcely surprising that the first important treatises on grace and free choice in Early Scholasticism come from the pen of Anselm, the Archbishop of Canterbury. Both at the beginning of his theological career with the well-known treatise *On Freedom of Choice* (c. 1080-85) and toward the end

29. Lottin, *Psychologie et morale au XIIe et XIIIe siècles* (Louvain-Gembloux, 1942-60), 6 Vols.; Landgraf, *Dogmengeschichte der Frühscholastik. Erster Teil. Die Gnadenlehre* (Regensburg, 1952-53), 2 Vols; and J. Auer, *Die Entwicklung der Gnadenlehre in der Hochscholastik* (Freiburg, 1951). Lonergan, *Grace and Freedom*, Chap. 1 gives a synthetic view.

30. Lottin claims that the nature of *liberum arbitrium* was the dominant problem until the middle of the thirteenth century when its place was taken by the analysis of liberty itself (*Psychologie et Morale*, Vol. 1, 12), though, of course, the problems cannot really be separated (Vol. 1, 223).

31. Lonergan, 16-9.

with his more mature *On the Harmony of the Foreknowledge, the Predestination and the Grace of God with Free Choice* (c. 1107-08), Anselm shows his fascination with these topics. His works are a programatic statement of many of the issues that were to exercise the wits of a generation of theologians: e.g., the definition of free choice, the explanation of Adam's freedom to sin and the freedom that remains in fallen man despite his inability to do good works, and finally, the determination of how the real freedom (or uprightness, as Anselm would say) of free will can only be restored by God. We must not be led to think, however, that Anselm's influence alone was responsible for the dominance of these problems. Wider factors—cultural, educational, and above all theological—were at work in its origin; Anselm's contribution was characteristically brilliant in isolating the problems, but questionable in its solutions. His views, especially his definition of *liberum arbitrium* from the point of view of final causality, as the ability to keep uprightness (*rectitudo*) of will for its own sake,[32] were to have a considerable following; but were never to be universally accepted. Furthermore, in Anselm's later treatise it should be noted that the first two parts are devoted to the abstract problems of foreknowledge, predestination, and contingency, an innovation that on the whole was not to be pursued by his immediate successors.

After Anselm's death in 1109, the banner of theological effort passed to the more conservative theologians associated with the Cathedral School at Laon, such as William of Champeaux and Anselm of Laon. Our evidence for the teaching of this School, fragmentary and of subsequent character as it is, indicates that the Laon theologians were more successful in appropriating the past than in making significant advances in the resolution of the problems involved.[33] Such appropriation of the complex heritage of Christian speculation on grace and free choice was necessary before a new stage could come into being. There is evidence to indicate that the de-

---

32. *De libertate arbitrii* 3; and *De concordia praescientiae et praedestinationis et gratia Dei cum libero arbitrio* 1:6 (*Sancti Anselmi Opera,* ed. F. Schmitt, Vol. 1, 212, Vol. 2, 256).

33. Lottin, 15-20.

cade of the 1120's saw such a new stage. The *De sententiis divinae paginae,* dependent on the writings of the Laon theologians and of uncertain date, distinguishes between three definitions of *liberum arbitrium,* that of Anselm, that of Augustine, and that of Boethius:[34] a sign of some maturity in the work of collation and comparison. But the most significant theological work of this decade on these problems was not a work of the Schools, but that of the "Last of the Fathers," Bernard of Clairvaux.[35]

A COMMENTARY ON BERNARD'S TREATISE

The Abbot of Clairvaux addresses the work to his close friend and theological companion, William, the abbot of St Thierry. The two had been friends for a decade or more and William had already produced some of the works which were to make him one of the most profound mystical theologians of the century. Bernard begs suggestions for emendations in this "obscure subject," but we have no idea of knowing how much William himself may have contributed to the process of correction.

Reference has already been made to Bernard's account of the situation which prompted the writing of the treatise. Bernard's questioner was obviously not a Semi-Pelagian: his difficulties appear to have related to the role of free will in the justified man, but the Abbot used the occasion of a query concerning a doctrine of good works and merit for a review in depth of all the ramifications of the connection of grace and freedom.

By way of anticipation, he begins with a brief summary (1:2) of the fundamental relationship between the two: there is a cooperation between grace and free choice, but all the initiative must be ascribed to grace. Nonetheless, the dignity of free choice is already manifest. If no one but God can grant salvation, nothing but free choice can receive it. "To

34. *Ibid.*
35. On Bernard's theological position in 1120's see J. Châtillon, "Influence de Saint Bernard sur la scolastique," *Saint Bernard Théologien,* 275-6.

consent is to be saved," and only free choice, not the natural appetite that man shares with the animals, is capable of this. The voluntary consent of which the Abbot speaks is then defined as "a self-determining habit of the soul," for where the will exists freedom must also be found. This identification of the will with the power of voluntary consent is capped by Bernard's assertion that this is what he means by "free choice."

Right at the outset of his treatise, then, the Abbot of Clairvaux declares his agreement with the tradition that finds in freedom the essence of the will.[36] This is why the remainder of the work will concentrate on the term *liberum arbitrium* rather than *voluntas* itself. Nevertheless, the Saint does wish to provide a firm basis for the understanding of free choice which he advances here. Hence in chapter two he turns to a clarification of the terms involved.[37]

In defining free choice Bernard makes use of none of the three classic definitions of the *De sententiis divinae paginae*: that of Boethius, "the free judgment concerning the will;" that of Augustine, "the power of doing good or evil;" and that of Anselm, "the faculty of preserving uprightness for its own sake."[38] It is a sign of the Abbot's independence of mind that he is ready to provide both his own definition and a framework within which to place it. He distinguishes life, sense-perception, natural appetite, and consent. The consent that he is speaking of here is further clarified as ". . . a spontaneous inclination of the will, or indeed, as I recall expressing it earlier, a self-determining habit of the soul." (2:3). At first glance, Bernard's definition has at least one major misleading aspect, that is the introduction of the term "habit." We must assume that the term is not to be taken in any technical sense, especially not in a strictly Aristotelian one, as

36. Venuta, *Libero Arbitrio,* 59, note 1, notes that Bernard does not even try to prove the existence of *liberum arbitrium* as Augustine had, but presupposes it as an inescapable datum of experience.

37. The most valuable commentary on this section is to be found in Venuta, Chap. 2, "Volontà, Ragione, e Libero Arbitrio," 44-69.

38. Lottin, 16.

Aquinas remarked.[39] In fact, everything that Bernard has to say about *liberum arbitrium* indicates that habit here merely means "a way of acting," and a way that is in no sense infused or acquired, but only expressed, as the actuation of the inamissable nature of man.[40] Consent, as A. Forest pointed out,[41] is not only assent to a particular course of action but the self-actuation of the created spirit—"self-determining" (*liber sui*) is the key term in the definition.

Bernard next turns to an analysis of the relation of will (*voluntas*) and reason (*ratio*) to the essence of consent or free choice. Twelfth-century thinkers were not unacquainted with the delicate problems of the relationship of intellect and will.[42] For the Abbot of Clairvaux will presides over and organizes sense-perception and appetite; but is itself a "rational movement" (*rationalis motus*). Thus, as G. Venuta has pointed out,[43] the two distinguishing characteristics of the Bernardine notion of the will are rationality and liberty. But how does Bernard actually conceive of reason's relation to the activity of the will? Some of Bernard's Scholastic successors interpreted him as holding that the act of judgment was subsequent to the act of the will rather than antecedent.[44] Nevertheless, it does seem that Bernard also admits an antecedent relation, as his emphasis on reason's instruction of the will indicates. There is much about the Abbot's doctrine here (2:3-5) that remains obscure and the subject of disagreement among his interpreters. Reason always accompanies the will, but the will does not always act from reason. "Indeed, it does many things through reason and against reason." This seems to suggest a true and false sense of reason,[45] and perhaps hint

39. *Summa* Ia, q. 83, a. 2, ad 2. Free choice in the Aristotelian sense, of course, is a potency rather than a habit.

40. Venuta, 59-62.

41. "Das Erlebnis," 121.

42. General studies, such as that of Bourke, can be misleading on this point; see his remarks on Bernard in *Will and Western Thought*, 82-3.

43. *Libero Arbitrio*, 48. On Bernard's doctrine of the will see also Hiss, *Die Anthropologie*, 132-7.

44. E.g., Richard Fishacre (died 1248) as cited in Lottin, 116. Bernard's description of reason as the *pedissequa* of *voluntas* probably had much to do with this.

45. Venuta, 55; and W. Williams, *The Treatise*, 8, note 3.

at a notion of an uprightness (*rectitudo*) of reason similar to that found in Anselm. Bernard appears to be saying that some kind of reason must accompany any act of the will, but that good acts of the will will be preceded by correct judgments. Nevertheless, he is true to the traditional Augustinian pattern in continuing to assert that the intellectual judgment cannot exercise necessary causality over the will; otherwise freedom would be an illusion (2:4). The speculative failure, however, is evident, since in neither case, that of good judgment or that of bad, is the nature of the relation really specified. It is not enough to say with G. Venuta that reason exercises some form of indirect action on the will.[46] As perspicacious as Bernard was in identifying the problems, he was no more successful than any other early twelfth-century author in working out the solutions.

A further complication is evident in the ambiguity with which Bernard treats the antecedent and subsequent roles of reason. The consent of the will is what makes man happy or unhappy and thus truly a man, and this consent is once again identified with free choice. "Such consent, I think, is well called free choice, on account of the imperishable freedom of the will and the inevitable judgment of the reason always and everywhere accompanying it, having free disposal of itself because of the will, and power to judge of itself because of the reason" (2:4). But the subsequent judgment which is then discussed is the judgment by which the will judges itself in the act of sinning (i.e. by its failure to be in conformity with eternal truth). Rhetorician to the core, the subtle wordplay between *arbitrium* and *iudicium* in which Bernard indulges in sections four and five of chapter two result in ambiguities of meaning that make it difficult at this juncture to be sure that we have a full grasp of his doctrine of the relation of intellect and will.

Bernard concludes by emphasizing the exclusion of necessity as the fundamental condition of freedom. Only the will in man possesses such freedom, and it alone is the source of

46. Venuta, 56.

merit and judgment (in the subsequent sense). The freedom that the will possesses is inalienable, it cannot be lost as long as the will is still a will. Bernard will return to the paradoxes of this doctrine in the later parts of the 'treatise. This freedom is based upon man's possession of rationality, since we can impute nothing to those who are not masters of their own reason, such as the mentally deficient, infants, and those who are sleeping. Thus, the role of reason, even if not still clear in many respects, is essential to free choice.

Chapter two of the *Grace and Free Choice,* along with the other passages where Bernard discusses the nature of *liberum arbitrium,*[47] raises the question of whether the *liberum arbitrium,* is primarily to be ascribed to the will, or to the intellect, or is perhaps to be taken as a separate faculty combining elements of the other two, as some later Scholastics did. We know that the status of *liberum arbitrium* was widely disputed during the Scholastic period,[48] and that Bernard was quoted in support of many opinions. Modern scholars have continued to disagree on Bernard's views. O. Lottin[49] and A. LeBail[50] hold that two equal elements, will and reason, are essential to Bernard's doctrine of *liberum arbitrium*; G. Venuta, after a careful consideration of all the texts, with rather more justice decides that the consent which is free choice belongs essentially to the will and that the accompaniment of the act of reason, while essential, is secondary.[51]

The most influential contribution of the entire treatise is introduced in the third chapter, the distinction of the three states of freedom. Due to its inclusion in the *Sentences* of Peter Lombard, it was to remain a familiar topic of discussion in the history of Scholasticism. Thomas Aquinas devoted an article to its defense in his earliest theological work, the *Com-*

47. E.g., 3:6; 4:11; and SC 81:6; OB 2:287-299.
48. Lottin, 11-224.
49. Lottin, 20.
50. Le Bail, c. 1461.
51. Venuta, 62-9, especially 65: "Si potrà cosi anche dire che, entitativamente, consenso e giudizio sono distinti, per attribuzione d'azione sono la stessa cosa." He cites Gilson in his support, *The Mystical Theology,* 50-1.

mentary on the Sentences (1252-54),[52] though in his later works he appears not to have found it useful.

The problem that led to the formulation of the states of liberty is an obvious one, and one that shows the dominant position of what we have called the historical complex of "sin-grace-freedom" in the thought of Bernard.[53] The Abbot of Clairvaux may have worked out a definition of free choice that he felt satisfactory, but as a believing Christian how could he square this definition with man's actual state after original sin? If the freedom to choose is so central to human nature that it cannot be compelled from without, how is it that fallen man is not free to choose the good? And does not the intervention of the grace necessary to perform a saving action make a mockery of man's so-called freedom? Are we not compelled by God?

Bernard's answer is to distinguish between various states of freedom. The Abbot's schema is drawn from key texts in the Pauline corpus. There is the freedom that Paul ascribes to the man who possesses the Spirit of the Lord in 2 Cor 3:17, and the "freedom from sorrow" of Rom 8:21. Neither of these can be identified with the freedom discussed in chapter two for which Bernard now coins the term "freedom from necessity," since this best expresses the voluntary character of free choice. The three freedoms are to be identified with the three diverse states of man: freedom from necessity belongs to our natural condition, freedom from sin to the life of grace, and freedom from sorrow to heaven (3:6-7).

The attempt to determine the various states of liberty was not original with Bernard; Augustine among others shows

---

52. *In II Sent.* d. 25, q. 1, a. 5.
53. There is no explicit appearance of the abstract schema in this treatise. McSorley, 134, following R. Mousnier, "St. Bernard and Luther," *American Benedictine Review,* 14 (1963), 460, claims that the Abbot recognized the distinction of types of necessity in SC 81:4—"Ergo quia volens, servam seipsam non modo *fecit,* sed *facit*" (OB 2:289). Bernard may have known of the distinction from its appearance in Anselm, but the very scarcity of its appearance and its lack of development indicate his preference for the concrete schema.

similar efforts. What does seem to be original is Bernard's formulation. In 1940 O. Lottin published a *Sententia de triplici libertate* connected with the School of Laon that was remarkably close to Bernard's position. In his new edition of the text in 1959,[54] he claimed that there was a serious probability that this sentence was authentically from Master Anselm.[55] Since the Laon scholar died in 1117, and since we know Bernard was friendly toward both him and his associate William of Champeaux this would seem to put the Abbot in the position of the borrower. E. Kleinedam, however, pointed out that the close verbal agreement of the texts is actually an argument in favor of Bernard's priority, since his habit is not to quote verbatim but to transform his sources.[56] Furthermore, the triple division does not appear in any of the early *Sentence* collections which can be definitively connected with Anselm,[57] and thus Bernard's origination of the division seems to be vindicated.[58]

In any case, far more important than the origin of the division is what Bernard was to do with it. Specifically, of what dogmatic advantage was it in correlating the teaching of Scripture and the Church on the states of freedom, and of what speculative use was it in explaining how fallen man's inability to choose the good does not destroy his radical liberty? By way of a preview of this analysis (which will occupy the next few chapters), Bernard emphasizes the role of Christ who alone among the sons of Adam possessed all three freedoms and therefore could serve as the liberator of free choice (3:7-8). Christ came to free the will not from necessity but from sin.

Bernard begins the analysis by a deeper exploration of

54. *Psychologie et Morale,* Vol. 5, 87. The text is found in Rouen ms. A. 307(626), f. 220v.

55. *Psychologie,* 82.

56. *"De triplici libertate . . .,"* *Cîteaux* 11 (1960): 60.

57. Ibid., 61.

58. Lottin himself has admitted Bernard's priority in the *Bulletin de théologie ancienne et médiévale,* 8 (1960), #1907; but claimed that the author of the *Sententia* did not copy from the Abbot himself, but from a resumé. Faust, in dependence on the work of J. Leclercq, holds that the *Sententia* does belong to the School of Laon, but is not from Anselm and therefore presumably posterior to Bernard. See "Bernhard's 'Liber de Gratia,' " 41-2.

freedom from necessity. At the beginning of his treatise *On Freedom of Choice,* Anselm of Canterbury had rejected the common definition of free choice as the ability to sin or not to sin since this would make it impossible for either God or the angels to be free.[59] Bernard adopts a similar position here. Just as the saints, angels, Christ, and God possess the fullness of the two final freedoms, so too they have perfect freedom from necessity. Indeed, freedom from necessity is unalterable: "Neither by sin nor by suffering is it lost or lessened; nor is it greater in the just man than in the sinner, nor fuller in the angel than in man" (4:9). The inalienability of free choice defined as the absence of external coercion is once more to the fore.[60]

However, while the essence of free choice remains unaltered, Bernard is willing to make some distinctions regarding the way in which it is possessed. It continues to exist even where the mind is captive to sin. Thus it is full (*plena*) in both good and bad men, but more orderly (*ordinatior*)[61] in the good, and more powerful in the Creator. Here again Bernard seems to show some echo of the Anselmian position on the uprightness of the will;[62] but, as usual, he is transforming his sources.[63]

The freedom from necessity which fallen man enjoys is not freedom from sin. Man's psychological consciousness of his

59. *De lib. arb.* 1 (ed., Vol. 1, 207).
60. The inalienable character of *liberum arbitrium* has led to some discussion concerning the status of the relation between liberty and the soul. After an extensive analysis, Venuta (82-3; 86) decided that *libertas* is a *proprium* of the soul for Bernard, i.e., a non-essential characteristic that is nonetheless inseparable. While there is no explicit reason for disagreeing with this position, it should be pointed out: (1) that Bernard displays no interest in such analysis himself; and (2) that Venuta's opinion is based more on SC 80-82 than upon our treatise.
61. The importance of the concept of order in the theology of Bernard has been pointed out by Standaert, "La doctrine de l'image," 71-2; and "Le principe de l'ordination dans la théologie spirituelle de Saint Bernard," *Collectanea Ordinis Cisterciensium Reformatorum,* 8 (1946): 178-216.
62. *De lib. arb.,* especially 3:13-4; and *De concordia* 1:6; and 3:3-4 (ed. Vol. 1, 210-3; 225-6; Vol. 2, 255-7; 265-8).
63. E. Gilson, *La liberté chez Descartes et la theologie* (Paris, 1913), 239-43, compares this passage with Descartes and suggests a source in Gregory of Nyssa.

desire for good and his inability to achieve it indicates that he does have a will (the faculty of desire), and will by definition must be free. He feels that freedom is captive to sin, not that it is lost. Only freedom from necessity, that by which the will can judge itself good or bad is of the essence of free choice. Freedom from sin is better called "free counsel" (*liberum consilium*), and freedom from sorrow "free counsel" (*liberum complacitum*). This new terminology for the triple division manifests the advantage which Bernard hopes to gain for the determination of how fallen man's inability to choose the good does not take away freedom. The key to the validity of the distinction in this area seems to rest on the difference between two intellectual operations, judgment and counsel. Original sin does not take away judgment, the ability to distinguish between right and wrong; counsel, on the other hand, that which determines ". . . the licit as more suitable and . . . the illicit as harmful" (4:11), is denied to fallen man. Neither of these intellectual acts can determine the will, for even the man who possesses grace and *liberum consilium* remains free to sin, but it is the lack of free counsel that is the cause of man's present sinfulness. "Now . . . we discern many things by means of the judgment as either to be done or omitted, which we nevertheless choose or reject through counsel in a manner quite at variance with the rectitude of our judgment (4:11)."[64] Bernard has here offered a clarification of his views on the relation of intellect and will. The antecedent role of intellect is to illuminate the will through a true *judgment,* i.e., one which possesses rectitude, and to show the will what is expedient and licit through free *counsel.* Because this latter is lacking in man since the Fall, he cannot choose the good, and hence the *judgment* subsequently judges his action as evil because of i. lack of conformity to truth.

Now the speculative nub of the argument is clear and it is one with which Christian theologians have continued to wres-

---

64. Bernard twice uses the Anselmian phrase *rectitudo iudicii,* here (ed. Vol. 3, 174, line 10) and in 6:17 (178, line 20). See Anselm's treatise *De veritate* 11 (ed. Vol. 1, 191). In 14:49, Bernard speaks of *rectitudo intentionis* (202, line 5).

tle. Granted that the loss of free counsel explains how it is easily possible for man to sin, does it mean that all of unredeemed man's actions are sinful, or is he capable of some actions which fulfill the law even if these are not saving actions? G. Venuta studied this question in the fourth chapter of his *Libero Arbitrio e Libertà della Grazia nel Pensiero di San Bernardo* and affirmed that Bernard, contrary to Augustine, admitted the possibility of virtuous actions among the pagans.[65] However, his position seems unwarranted, for first of all, however much this may seem to be a logical conclusion from what we have just seen, Bernard does not discuss the question explicitly; and secondly, the ability to draw the logical conclusion seems very much dependent on a clear distinction between natural and supernatural virtues that was not available in Bernard's time. Free choice is free for Bernard, but free only to sin.

The triple division of freedom does provide the Abbot of Clairvaux with a definite dogmatic advantage at the end of chapter four. Man's progress from the depths of sin to the glory of heaven is well illuminated by the division. Sunk in sin he possesses only freedom from necessity; he regains, partially but progressively, freedom of counsel through grace, though this cannot be perfectly achieved in this life. Free choice is in captivity to sin to some extent as long as full free counsel is not present. When this is restored in heaven it will be accompanied by the freedom from sorrow that God and the angels enjoy. At the very end of the chapter Bernard introduces an extraneous but typical note by blaming the intellect's weakness at least partially upon its association with the body.[66]

65. Venuta, 103-8; 125-7. Venuta's argument is that the inability of fallen man to fulfill the *whole* natural law affirmed in *De diligendo Deo* 2:6 suggests that he can at least fulfill part of it. But in that passage Bernard seems to be talking more about the impossibility of the total conversion of the will necessary to perform *any* good action. Bavaud, "Les rapports" 337, agrees that the Abbot makes no distinction between the aid that God gives to perform naturally good actions and that which he bestows for supernatural ones.

66. He cites Wis 9:15 in support of this view. The text appears frequently in the treatise, especially in the later chapters; it was also used by a number of other Cistercians, e.g., Isaac of Stella, *Epistola de anima* (PL 194:1875C).

Chapter five briefly examines how far freedom from sorrow and freedom from sin may exist in this world. Freedom from sorrow, or free pleasure, can scarcely be said to be found among men: even virtue does not bring freedom from pain, and the pleasure of vice, false joy that it is, is the most abject sorrow. The pleasure of the goods of the body is unstable, and only the variation between degrees of sorrow may be said to provide some natural joy. True joy is occasionally tasted only in the excess of contemplation,[67] while freedom from sin, or free counsel, is possessed in some degree by all the righteous.

One of the key tensions of the concrete historical complex, that of the relation between sin and freedom reaches its deepest expression in chapter six. Supplementing and deepening positions taken earlier, Bernard fleshes out the concept of the "captivity of free choice" which he mentioned in four. Free choice is captive as long as it is not accompanied by the fullness of the other two freedoms. "To will lies in our power indeed as a result of free choice, but not to carry out what we will" (6:16).[68] In dependence on Paul and Augustine, Bernard now arrives at a deeper explanation of man's inability to achieve good than that manifested by the loss of *liberum consilium*. Not only the intellect, but also the will has been affected by original sin: the will can will, but it cannot will the achievement which is the good; it can only will the bad, the defect that springs from itself. This confirms our conclusion that *liberum arbitrium* alone cannot perform naturally good actions.

But does not such a position effectively destroy real free choice? Bernard, and it must be admitted a number of important Christian theologians from Augustine on, seem to think not.[69] The Abbot says that the essence of freedom is to

67. On the doctrine of *excessus* which Bernard took from Maximus the Confessor, see Gilson, *The Mystical Theology,* 25-8.

68. On the importance of the difference between the will and its efficacy in the Middle Ages see Gilson, *The Spirit of Mediaeval Philosophy,* 316-8.

69. McSorley, 25-9, making use of Adler's survey speaks of three kinds of freedom: natural, circumstantial, and acquired. He claims that what Bernard is speaking of here is only natural freedom, " . . . man's ability to choose and to make decisions" (p. 367), not the power to carry out what he chooses (pp. 133-4).

be affirmed or denied from the point of view of the willing subject and not from that of the willed object. In other words, where we have a subject acting spontaneously and free from external coercion, we have free choice.[70] The eminently theological character of Bernard's notion of freedom is highlighted by the distinction he calls in here to illuminate the gap between will and performance. Creating grace (*gratia creans*) is responsible for the existence of the free subject; saving grace *gratia salvans* for its achievement;[71] or in terms of the will, from the former we have the simple ability of will, from the latter the ability to will the good (6:16).[72] Hearkening back to another notion introduced earlier, Bernard also identifies the action of saving grace with the "ordering" of the affections and will given by creating grace.[73] Virtues then are nothing more than "ordered affections," and it is Christ who enables us to order them (6:17).

Like Augustine,[74] Bernard goes on to refuse to admit that free will has perpetual indifference after the Fall. We must belong either to the devil or to God, i.e., our actions must spring either from *caritas* or from *cupiditas*. Nonetheless, when we belong to either God or Satan, we are still our own,

70. As Venuta has pointed out (p. 79) or these two characteristics, one positive and the other negative, are the essential attributes of freedom for Bernard. The Italian scholar's summary of the characteristics of liberty on 86-7 is worth noting. The two fundamental aspects of "non-necessity and spontaneity" and "liberty and will" result in the "accidentality-inseparability" of liberty's relation to the will. The final aspect is that of the "universality-integrity" of liberty in thinking subjects.

71. This distinction was fairly popular in the twelfth century; and, although it is generally Augustinian in character, Bernard's adoption may have had something to do with its popularity. We find it in a number of authors influenced by him, e.g., Hugh of St Victor, *De sacramentis* 1, 6:17 (PL 176:273CD); Isaac of Stella, *Sermo 26 in Sexagesima* and *Epistola de anima* (PL 194:1774D-75D; 1887D); and Richard of St Victor, *Liber exceptionum* 2:1 (ed. Châtillon, 114).

72. The formula "Itaque liberum arbitrium nos facit volentes, gratia benevolos" (ed. 178, lines 3-4) is fundamentally Augustinian, e.g., *Sermo 156* (PL 38:856).

73. P. Delfgaauw, "La nature et les degres de l'amour selon Saint Bernard," *Saint Bernard Théologien*, 235-51, discusses the ordering of the affections. On the importance of this passage for Bernard's views on *ordinatio*, cf. Standaert, "Le principe de l'ordination," 188-90.

74. See Teselle, *Augustine the Theologian*, 291-3, for a good summary of Augustine's refusal to admit complete indifference as the essential note of freedom.

though with the significant difference that when we belong to Satan our own will is the cause, but when we belong to God the cause is his grace (6:18).[75]

The last two sections (19-20) of this important chapter fill out the implications of the prevenience of grace for the other two kinds of freedom that Bernard has distinguished. Perfect willing, i.e., the final stage beyond that of willing the good, needs a twofold gift of grace: true wisdom (*verum sapere*), which is what signifies the conversion of the will to the good, and full power (*plenum posse*), which is the confirmation in the good whose perfection can only be achieved in the next life. True wisdom here is described in terms of the effect it produces on the will; but, as Bernard's language shows, and as he later affirms, it informs the *consilium* of the intellect which enables man to do what is fitting.[76] Free counsel is the freedom to do the good. Conversion is the perfecting goodness of the will that builds upon the general goodness that it possesses as a part of creation and the special goodness freedom of choice has as the image of God. For Bernard total conversion, the complete ordering of intellect and will which he has often mentioned,[77] and perfect righteousness are all one and the same; and because they involve the fullness of glory they cannot be ascribed to anyone in this life, not even to Adam, for had he possessed them how could he have sinned?

It is not Bernard's purpose to write a treatise on original sin, but the doctrine of free choice he has expounded and the analysis of the states of freedom he has sketched make it necessary for him to take Adam's original condition into con-

75. Williams, 32, note 1, points to affinities here with Augustine's *De natura et gratia* 23:25 (CSEL 60,251).

76. Compare 4:11 (" . . . ita per consilium et *licita,* tamquam *commoda,* nobis *eligere* . . .," ed., 174, lines 2-3) with 6:19 (" . . . ut nil *libeat* nisi quod *deceat* vel *liceat,*" 180, lines 10-1). On the equation between *verum sapere* and *liberum consilium* see Venuta, 117-21, who points out how the *sapientia* which Bernard speaks of here is Augustinian in its involvement of intellect and will.

77. 6:19 (ed., 180, lines 19-21) gives an admirable definition of the *ordinatio* of the will: " . . . omnimodo conversio voluntatis ad Deum, et ex tota se voluntaria devotaque subiectio." On total conversion as *ordinatio,* see Standaert, "Le principe de l'ordination," 202.

sideration. The dilemma in which the Abbot finds himself is that if Adam possessed only freedom of choice, what did he lose in being expelled from paradise? If, on the other hand, he also possessed freedom of counsel and of pleasure, how did he come to sin? The answer given to this problem is directly dependent upon St Augustine who in his work *On Rebuke and Grace* had distinguished between . . . "to be able not to sin, and not to be able to sin. . . ."[78] Bernard uses this to show the grades that exist in freedom of counsel and freedom of pleasure. "The higher freedom of counsel consists in not being able to sin, the lower in being able not to sin. Again, the higher freedom of pleasure lies in not being able to be disturbed, the lower in being able not to be disturbed" (7:21). The fall of man was a fall into not being able not to sin and not being able not to be disturbed. This fall took place through the power of free choice, a power that man had been given for his glory, but had used for his own condemnation. Man had been given the ability to stand in his first state, but, since his gifts were only the lower grades of freedom of counsel and freedom of pleasure, he was not given the ability to rise again. Free choice, though it remains free, is now entrapped. The admirable dogmatic precision of Bernard's triple distinction for the presentation of the Pauline and Augustinian heritage is evident in these succinct and clear summaries.

The state of not being able not to sin does not put an end to free choice, it only means that the free counsel by which man possessed the wisdom and the free pleasure by which he had the power not to sin have been removed. Free choice is only responsible for making a creature willing, not for making it wise or powerful. Free choice remains in both the good and the bad, as long as they possess a will (8:24). The question might occur as to why free choice is not able to regain

---

78. 12:33 (PL 44:936). Translation from *The Nicene and Post-Nicene Fathers,* Series 1, Vol 5, 485. On the influence of chapters 11, 12, and 14 of the *De correptione et gratia* on this chapter of Bernard, see Faust, 44-5. Landgraf, *Dogmengeschichte,* Vol, 1, 102, mentions the discussion of the three states of man in the *Contra Eutychen* (ed., 122-6) of Boethius as a possible source.

the state that it lost. Bernard, basing himself on the fact that all these states are free gifts of God, shows that it is impossible for man to rise on his own. If Adam before the Fall could not of his own power ascend from the lower to the higher degrees of free counsel and free pleasure, *a fortiori* this is true of our own chance of regaining some measure of these freedoms. Only Christ, "the power of God and the wisdom of God" (1 Cor 1:24), can work the restoration of man's free pleasure and free counsel. Naturally, the perfection of these two, i.e., their higher stages, must wait for the next life.[79] Freedom of counsel enables us not to give way to sin, though we cannot be free of it completely; freedom of pleasure enables us not to fear adversity for the sake of righteousness (8:25-26). The process of learning from free counsel not to abuse free choice in order one day to enjoy full freedom of pleasure is the reparation of the image of God in us (8:27).

Bernard's doctrine of the image of God, outlined in chapter nine, has occasioned much discussion. This is not because the doctrine of the treatise is itself obscure; it is rather that Bernard appears to have held different doctrines at other times.[80] Consequently, the best procedure for the sake of our task seems to be to comment on the position adopted here and then to append a brief discussion of the problems introduced by the other texts.

The image and the likeness of God in which man was created (Gen 1:26) is to be found in the three freedoms. Free choice, because of its unchangeableness has imprinted upon it "some substantial image of the eternal and immutable

---

79. In 5:15, Bernard had held that " . . . on this earth, contemplatives alone can in some way enjoy freedom of pleasure, though only in part . . ." This must refer to the higher freedom of pleasure, if we wish to avoid a contradiction with the present passage which affirms a share in the freedom of pleasure for all the saved here below.

80. For a general approach to the doctrine of the image of God in the twelfth-century theology see S. Otto, *Die Funktion des Bildbegriffes in der Theologie des 12. Jahrhunderts* (*Beiträge zur Geschichte der Philosophie und Theologie des Mittelalters,* 40:1, Münster, 1963); and R. Javelet, *Image et ressemblance au douzième siècle* (Paris, 1967), 2 Vols. For a treatment of Bernard's views, cf. 283-4 in Otto; and Vol. 1, 189-97 in Javelet.

deity."[81] Since free counsel and free pleasure are both subject to diminution or loss they form the accidental likeness (*similitudo*) of divine power and wisdom (9:28) This observation concerning the degrees of free counsel and free pleasure leads the Abbot to introduce a clarification of his earlier doctrine on the freedoms: instead of the two degrees, e.g., "able not to sin" and "not able to sin," we are now given three, because Adam's ability not to sin was higher and more perfect than our own, without however attaining to the state of not being able to sin which God and the angels enjoy (9:29).[82] Lastly, the Saint turns his attention to the fate of the freedoms in hell. Scripture itself indicates that both freedom of counsel and freedom of pleasure vanish in hell, whereas freedom of choice, as has been frequently pointed out, remains unchanged. Bernard refutes the objection that souls in hell gain some wisdom from the punishment they suffer by distinguishing between the sinful act and bad will—such souls certainly repent of sinful actions, but their evil wills remain the same.

Chapter ten continues the discussion by summarizing Bernard's doctrine on the restoration of the likeness lost through sin. Likeness is restored to man and the stain removed from his image only through the activity of Christ. One noteworthy point in the allegorical interpretation of the parable of the woman with the lost coin of Luke's Gospel that he uses as an illustration here is the introduction of the term "the region of unlikeness" to describe the state of fallen man. Since its notice by E. Gilson,[83] the history of this term (which takes its remote origin in Plato's *Statesman* 273d but whose major source for the Middle Ages was Augustine's

81. Standaert, "La doctrine de l'image," 76-7, rightly finds some ambiguity in this doctrine. If what the image consists in is its inalienability and share in the eternity of God, which comes first? "Le libre arbitre est-il image parce qu'il est inamissible, ou est-il inamissible, parce qu'il est image?" Both Standaert and Venuta (40) suggest that the latter supposition is more likely.

82. Bernard interprets the scriptural passage "No one born of God commits sin" (1 Jn 3:19) as proof for the fact that from the point of view of predestination the sins that the just commit do not interfere with the glory that they shall enjoy hereafter.

83. *The Mystical Theology*, 45, 115-7, 205, and 223-4.

Confessions 7, 10, 16) has been the subject of extensive examination. Bernard's use probably had much to do with its popularity in the twelfth century, particularly among Cistercians.[84] Christ's position as the "Form" of the Godhead explains how he unites the functions of creator and redeemer. Bernard's lapidary expression could not be bettered: "That very form came, therefore, to which free choice was to be conformed, because in order that it might regain its original form, it had to be reformed from that out of which it had been formed" (10:33).[85] Conformation means that the image should do the same thing in its small world, the body, as the Form, Divine Wisdom, does in the large world of the universe,[86] i.e., it should rule each sense and each member in a way that will prevent sin from reigning. When he is freed from sin, man begins to recover his freedom of counsel and a likeness worthy of the divine image (10:34). Nevertheless, Bernard closes his discussion of man as the image and likeness of God by emphasizing that it is to be understood according to the major lines of the whole treatise. We are not to think that the image, that is, free choice, possesses this power of conformation of itself. This would be to suppose that the essence of free choice rests in the ability to choose good or evil, and Bernard again agrees with Anselm that this view shows its falsity by denying free will to God, the devil, the angels, the saints, and the damned. The Abbot summarily shows once again how free choice as a spontaneous willing free of external coercion must be predicated of God, the devil, and man.

Such is the view of image and likeness found in the *Grace*

84. For a survey of its use in the twelfth century and an introduction to the rich bibliography on the topic see Javelet, *Image et Ressemblance,* Vol. 1, 266-85.

85. On Bernard's doctrine of *forma* here Standaert notes: "Peut-être faut-il dire que *forma* désigne une perfection, ou la perfection d'un être; dans la creature elle est essentiellement participation de la perfection divine, qui crée la perfection finie, et en consitutue l'exemplaire" ("La doctrine de l'image," 118).

86. The text that Bernard used here (Wis 8:1) was later taken up by Isaac of Stella in a similar microcosmic sense in his *Epistola* (PL 194:1885D). On the history of microcosmic themes see R. Allers, "Microcosmos from Anaximandros to Paracelsus," *Traditio,* 2 (1944), 319-409. On microcosmic texts in Bernard, cf. Hiss, *Die Anthropologie,* 72-3, note 16.

and Free Choice. Unfortunately for the neatness of Bernard's doctrine, he could not refrain from discussing image and likeness on a number of other occasions.[87] In the treatise *On Loving God,* probably written slightly before *Grace and Free Choice,* he holds that of the three goods belonging to the soul, (dignity, knowledge, and virtue), it is the first, dignity, which is to be equated with the free choice through which man is said to be made in the image and likeness of God.[88] This rather vague treatment is not unreconcilable with the *Grace and Free Choice,* which still used the word "dignity" to refer to free choice.[89] There are, however, many later texts, some datable and others not, in which quite differing treatments appear. To show their distance from the earlier view it is sufficient to take a look at the most noted, that found in Sermons 80 to 82 of the *Sermons On the Song of Songs* (probably written about 1148).[90] In these Sermons, the soul no longer bears the image of God itself, but is made "to the image" of the true Image who is the Word.[91] This image is said to consist in greatness (*magnitudo*) and uprightness (*rectitudo*).[92] Likeness now is described as threefold, consisting in simplicity, immortality, and free choice.[93] As many have remarked, this leads to an inversion of the view adopted in the earlier treatise, since it is the image now which is lost, at least in part, by sin, and the likeness that is permanent.[94] Bernard himself was conscious of the difference (though perhaps not as conscious as the modern student might have liked), since he closes Sermon 81 with the enig-

87. For Bernard's doctrine of image and likeness, besides the general works, already mentioned, cf. Gilson, *The Mystical Theology,* 46-59; Hiss, *Die Anthropologie,* 66-89; Venuta, 37-43; and especially the excellent survey of Standaert, "La doctrine de l'image."

88. *De Diligendo Deo* 2:2-6 (OB 3:121-124). See Standaert, 74-5. Venuta, 38, claims that in this first Bernardine position free choice equals both image and likeness.

89. E.g., 11:36 (OB 3:191, lines 5-10).

90. On these texts see Standaert, 85-90; and Venuta, 41-3.

91. SC 80:2 (OB 2:277-8).

92. SC 80:5 (OB 2:280-1).

93. SC 81:3 (OB 2:286-8).

94. E.g., Javelet, *Image et ressemblance,* Vol. 1, 195. On 196-7 Javelet notes the influence of William of St Thierry on Bernard's doctrine.

matic statement: "In the treatise which I wrote on *Grace and
Free Choice,* are to be read discussions that are perhaps
different on the image and likeness, but not, as I think, oppo-
site. You have read those, you have heard these; whichever
are to be more favored, I leave to your judgment."[95]

It is not necessary, even were there the space, to survey all
the other variations in Bernard's teaching on image and likeness to agree with the judgment of M. Standaert that the
Abbot has not one but several doctrines on this question.[96]
Nevertheless, there is truth in Bernard's remark about *diversa
sed non adversa* if we give the word "doctrine" a somewhat
generous meaning, for there is an important common element, a quality of relatedness, in all the things that he had to
say about man as God's image and likeness.[97] For our purposes, at least, it is enough to note both the clarity of that
aspect of Bernard's views exposed in the *Grace and Free
Choice* and its perfect comformability with the rest of the
treatise, whatever variations he was to offer at a later time.[98]

Finally, the distinctive character of Bernard's views on man
as the image and likeness of God should be emphasized. As E.
Gilson has shown,[99] while both Augustine and Bernard place
the image of God in man's spiritual nature, Bernards differs

95. SC 81:11 (OB 2:291, lines 13-6). The key phrase in the Latin reads " ... *diversa* fortassis de imagine et similitudine disputata leguntur, sed, ut arbitror, *non
adversa.*"

96. "La doctrine de l'image," 100. In fact, he holds that there are four doctrines
in all: those of the formulations of Gra and SC, as well as the irreducible difference between the concept of the soul as the image of the Trinity and that of the
soul as the image-imprint (p. 101).

97. Standaert has vindicated this (102-4, 121), finding the common element in
the notion of man as *capax Dei,* and the variation at least partially based upon the
Scriptural multiplicity of the theme. Hiss, 76-77, also holds for a basic unity,
though he bases it upon man's superiority over all other creatures.

98. Javelet, *Image et ressemblance*, Vol. 1, 196-7, speculates that the change in
the SC is due to the influence of William of St Thierry. J. Danielou holds that it
was the authority of Gregory of Nyssa's *De hominis opificio* to which William
drew Bernard's attention that was responsible. Cf. "St. Bernard et les pères grecs,"
Saint Bernard Théologien, 52-5. In this he is followed by M. Canevet, "Gregoire
de Nysse," *Dictionnaire de Spiritualité* (Paris, 1967), Vol. 6, c. 1008. Danielou
further asserts the possibility of some influence of Gregory on Gra, but admits
that the comparisons he draws are very general.

99. *The Spirit of Mediaeval Philosophy*, 210-3.

from his great predecessor in stressing human freedom rather than human intellection as the precise *locus* of the image. The variations in Bernard's own views and the richness of the doctrine in both the Abbot of Clairvaux and the Bishop of Hippo indicate that their views should be seen as complementary rather than opposed, another case of *diversa sed non adversa*.

The eleventh and twelfth chapters form a unit, as do the thirteenth and fourteenth. The first unit revolves around what might be considered difficulties concerning the inalienability of free choice. In this unit chapter eleven serves as a general introduction and chapter twelve considers some classic examples. Neither grace nor temptation take away free choice because God, by sharing his dignity with man, allows the creature to become good (by cooperation with his grace) or evil (through his own fault). God does not take away free will when he converts man, but transfers its allegiance. The Scriptural texts concerning temptation which seem to undermine freedom actually do not touch free choice. Even the captivity to sin of which Paul complains (Rom 7:23) is really the lack of full freedom of counsel, and other Pauline texts are adduced to demonstrate the Apostle's consciousness of his freedom of choice.

Chapter twelve considers the standard objection against the Bernardine theory of will as complete voluntareity, viz., that external coercion is sometimes so strong that free choice seems to be impossible. As befits a theological treatise the example used is a Scriptural one, that of Peter's denial, and in this Bernard seems to express some dependence again on Augustine's *On Rebuke and Grace*.[100] It might be said that those who through fear of death deny their faith either contract no guilt by making a merely verbal denial or are forced to do what they do not will and thus are equally innocent, free choice having perished. Bernard will have none of this: the nature of the will is not such as to admit contrary volitions at the same time. Nonetheless, he recognized the prob-

---

100. 9:24 (PL 44:931) considers the case of Peter. Faust, 47-8, holds that the dependence is only general.

lem. Peter, for example, did not wish to deny Christ, and therefore it seems that his tongue was moved against his will. What Peter wanted all along was to remain a disciple of Christ's. His will never changed. The objection is put with great rhetorical force, so that Bernard has to try to outdo himself in responding. The key to the answer is given in the objector's admission of two wills in Peter. At first sight, they both appear blameless—the desire to avoid death and joy in being Christ's disciple. However, these are not the two wills that are really in conflict—the real war is expressed in the dilemma "either to lie or to die," and in choosing to lie Peter has preferred the good of the body over that of the soul, an obvious lack to the uprightness of truth in Bernard's hierarchical view of values. The ultimate perduring will in Peter then was not that of remaining a disciple of Christ, as the objector imagined; but in loving himself to excess. The test merely made this free choice evident (12:38).

One might have thought that Bernard had proved his point. Our tastes are not those of the twelfth century, though, and the Abbot's rather long digression on the paradoxes of the "willy-nilly" (12:39-41), however tedious to us, was probably much appreciated by his first readers. To be brief: though it may be true to say that the will is forced, it can be forced by nothing other than itself. Bernard distinguishes two kinds of compulsion, the passive compulsion which can occur without the consent of the sufferer, and the active compulsion which we exert on ourselves.[101] Active compulsion is when the will is prevailed upon to will something which would not happen if we did not will it. Consequently, it is ours and we are responsible for it. In conclusion, the Abbot returns to the fundamentals of his doctrine: free choice, or human will, is located between the divine Spirit and the fleshly appetite. In its present historical state its inclinations are all toward the fleshly appetite; without the assistance of the Spirit it can do nothing. But it is still free.

101. See Venuta, 74-5. Interestingly, Bernard gives no examples of varieties of active compulsion nor of passive. One of the real weaknesses in his theory of the will is the great difficulty it has in dealing with questions of mitigated responsibility. A Bernardine manual of casuistry would surely be a slim book.

The final two chapters of the *Grace and Free Choice* concern the relation between the will of God and man's free
decision in the saving act.[102] Here the Abbot returns to the
question posed by his interrogator at the beginning of the
treatise: he thus seems to suggest that only on the basis of a
nuanced doctrine of human freedom can one understand
what part belongs to free choice and what part to grace in the
work of salvation.[103] Bernard's teaching throughout chapter
thirteen is deeply Augustinian. Following his usual practice,
he rarely cites explicitly; but his dependence on Augustine,
especially on the Bishop's own *Grace and Free Choice* treatise is unmistakable.[104]

Making clear that he is not speaking of the special case of
original sin, Bernard reiterates the doctrine with which we
have now become familiar: free choice is either justly condemned because of its own fault, or freely saved through the
mercy of God. The gifts of God are to be divided into merits,
which are our own in the present life, and rewards which
shall be granted to us hereafter. Both, however, have God as
their ultimate source, for ". . . both our works and his rewards are undoubtedly God's gifts, and he who placed himself in our debt by his gifts, constituted us by our works real
deservers" (13:43).[105] The exact nature of merits, those acts
in which God decides to make use of the ministry of creatures, needs further investigation. Bernard distinguishes three
modes of God's activity upon creatures to specify what he
means by merit. God can act "through the creature yet without it" (*per creaturam sine ipsa*), "through the creature but
against it" (*per creaturam contra ipsam*), or "through the
creature and with it" (*per creaturam cum ipsa*). The first type
of activity pertains to the use that God makes of insensible

102. For an outline of Bernard's doctrine in chapters 13 and 14 see Venuta,
chap. 6 "La cooperazione," 137-60.
103. Venuta summarizes: "Ma il suo problema centrale è questo: che cosa fa il
libero arbitrio e che cosa fa la grazia nella salvezza dell'uomo? " (159).
104. The best discussion of the Augustinian sources of the chapter is in Faust,
48-50.
105. Faust compares this with Augustine's *De gratia et libero arbitrio* 21:43 (PL
44:909).

and irrational creatures in his eternal salvific plan; the second to the way in which he uses evil agents for his own good purposes.[106] Only the last illustrates the category of merit, i.e., those activities where God ordains the good will of angels or men to have the privilege of cooperating with his plan (13:44). In all three cases we are dealing with instrumental causes, but only in the third is there a question of merit, as Paul himself has affirmed. There alone does God's gift of voluntary consent allow us to say that we are his fellow-workers.

Chapter fourteen follows up this general picture by determining in greater detail just where the action of grace works alone and where it deigns to associate human activity with itself. Again taking his cue from Paul and Augustine, the Abbot distinguishes three moments in the good act: ". . . thinking, willing, and accomplishing the good; the first he does without us; the second, with us; and the third, through us."[107] *Bona cogitatio,* obviously the effective cause of free counsel, is the realm of purely prevenient grace—where God acts neither through us nor with us (*nec per nos . . . , nec nobiscum*). In changing our evil will to consent to him and giving this consent the ability to perform the outward action God works without us but through us.[108] Only the middle stage, however, where he works with us, is that wherein man can gain merit. An action may give good example, but if it proceeds from some source other than a good intention, say fear or hypocrisy, it obviously can merit no-

---

106. Augustine treats of the use that God makes of evil wills in *De gratia et libero arbitrio,* (PL 44:907) 20:41; and in the *Enchiridion,* 101 (PL 40:279). Standaert, "Le principe de l'ordination," 197-8, shows the importance of this threefold use of creatures for Bernard's thought.

107. 14:46. The texts from Paul that Bernard is using here are Phil 2:13; Rom 7:18; and 2 Cor 3:5. While less developed than Bernard, Augustine strikes a similar note in *De gratia et libero arbitrio,* 17:33: "He operates, therefore, without us, in order that we may will; but when we will, and so will that we may act, he co-operates with us" (PL 44:901; translation from *The Nicene and Post-Nicene Fathers,* Series 1, Vol. 5, 458). Venuta, 142-3, note 2, points out that this triple division differs somewhat from the two given at the very beginning of the treatise.

108. Venuta, 142-9, has a good treatment of Bernard's doctrine concerning prevenient grace.

thing. *Bona cogitatio* arouses the soul, *bona actio* gives good example, only the *bona intentio* of *consensus* merits. The action of grace upon free choice is described as arousing, healing, strengthening, and saving; in the first case alone is its action prevenient. Bernard goes on to clarify the nature of the cooperation that grace elicits from free choice by stressing that: "It is not as if grace did one half of the work and free choice the other; but each does the whole work, in its own peculiar contribution. Grace does the whole work, and so does free choice—with this one qualification: that whereas the whole is done *in* free choice, so is the whole done *of* grace." (14:47). The admirable clarity of the Abbot of Clairvaux's dogmatic statement of the relation of *gratia cooperans* and free choice has been praised by many.[109] It illustrates both the strengths and the limitations of the treatise: on the one hand, precise doctrinal clarification; on the other, the absence of a speculative explanation of the nature of such cooperation due to Bernard's lack of an evolved notion of the will and theory of causality.[110]

Bernard goes on to show that what he has been describing is nothing other than what the Apostle was speaking of in the famous text from Romans: "So it depends not upon man's will or exertion, but upon God's mercy" (Rom 9:16). Creation, healing or justification, and ultimate salvation (perseverence in grace) are all completely the work of God and not of free will. We ignore God's righteousness if we imagine that our merits proceed from any other source but grace (14:48). Divine action in relation to free choice is threefold: creation, reformation, and consummation. All these are accomplished through the agency of Christ; in all, the divine activity must come first. Only reformation, that which produces the spirit of freedom,[111] involving our voluntary consent, is done with

---

109. E.g., Venuta, 152-3.

110. Faust, 49, also notes Bernard's lack of a doctrine of analogy.

111. For a study of the term *spiritus libertatis* (2 Cor 3:17) in Bernard's writings see A. Dimier, "Pour la fiche *spiritus libertatis*," *Revue du moyen âge latin*, 3 (1947), 56-60.

us (*nobiscum*) and is the source of merit. Bernard has now established the dogmatic principle at the center of the good works of the monastic life, and can thus reply to the implication of his questioner. Good works are valuable since they are the means by which our inner nature is renewed from day to day. Again, the Abbot appeals to Paul to show that such works are both God's gifts in that they come from grace, as well as our own merits, since they involve consent on our part. Cooperation alone is the root of merit (14:49-50).

One final problem remains to be clarified. If the will on which all merit depends is a gift of God (both as will itself by creation and as good will be reformation), how is it possible that Paul can speak of a crown of righteousness being laid up for *him* (2 Tim 4:7)? The answer, of course, is that the righteousness in question is not Paul's but God's; this righteousness is nothing other than the promise by which God has freely bound himself to reward those whom he associates with himself in the work of salvation. The just man, then, does not trust in his own merits, but in the promise of God, a note which has been sounded over and over again in the history of the Christian theology of grace and freedom, not least of all by the great voices of the Reformation. On this point the Abbot of Clairvaux ends his treatise.[112]

THE IMPORTANCE OF THE TREATISE IN THE HISTORY OF CHRISTIAN THOUGHT

It is not our place to attempt a complete evaluation of the influence that Bernard's *Grace and Free Choice* was to have on later Christian theology, but some notes concerning this history will be of help in estimating its significance.

Basic to the historical context in which the Abbot found himself was the differentiation of the tasks of theology, the fundamental significance of the development of the Scholastic method.[113] One important part of this differentiation

---

112. For an outline of the system of the treatise see the chart given at the end of this "Introduction."

113. See B. Lonergan, *Method in Theology* (N.Y., 1972), 138-40.

was the emergence of a clearly-defined and fully-mature speculative moment in the theological operation; this emergence
was something which slowly came to maturity during the
century and a half following Bernard's work. To say that
Bernard's treatise is primarily dogmatic is not to deny him an
important role in this speculative evolution. The Abbot of
Clairvaux was not opposed to Scholasticism as such; his close
association with the theologians of the school of Laon, the
influence that St Anselm exercised upon him, his friendship
with Hugh of St Victor, Peter Lombard, and others, are evidence enough against this.[114] He was merely opposed to what
he rightly or wrongly thought of as aberrations of the use of
reason in theology. Many of the questions which Bernard
discussed in this work were to be central to the development
of later speculation on grace and freedom, especially the definition of free choice, the distinction of various kinds of freedom, and the discussion of operative and cooperative grace
and their relation to merit. Without attempting any detailed
comparisons, it is still instructive to point out some of the
broad lines of this influence. J. Châtillon is undoubtedly correct in claiming that as far as the Scholastics were concerned
the *Grace and Free Choice* was the most influential of all
Bernard's works.[115]

As we have seen, the Abbot's triple distinction of the states
of liberty was apparently almost immediately seized upon as
one of the clearest and most orthodox solutions to a common theological concern. Not only was it copied almost
word-for-word in the *Sententia de triplici libertate,* but it also
appears in the *Summa Sententiarum,* an influential work

---

114. For the abbot's relations with the Scholastics, besides Châtillon, "Influence de S. Bernard sur le scolastique," see also R. Martin, ' La formation théolo-
gique de Saint Bernard," *Saint Bernard et son temps* (Dijon, 1928), 234-40. See
Bernard's EP 410 (PL 182:619A) for his relations with Odo of Lucca and Peter
Lombard.

115. "Influence de Saint Bernard sur le scholastique," 280-1: "Le *De gratia et
libero arbitrio* dont les définitions et les analyses apportaient à la psychologie et à
la morale des donées vraiment neuves, reste toujours l'ouvrage le plus fréquem-
ment cité et le plus constamment utilisé."

probably written shortly before 1140 by Bernard's friend Bishop Odo of Lucca.[116] Both the *Ysagoge in Theologiam,* a product of the School of Peter Abelard dating from the 1140's and the famous *Libri Sententiarum* of Peter Lombard (c. 1152) make use of the distinction, though they appear to know it through the version found in the *Summa Sententiarum.*[117] Naturally, its appearance in the Lombard's *Sentences* guaranteed it quite an extensive later history, though many authors knew of the distinction directly through Bernard. We also find the triple distinction used by the Abbot's followers in the Order of Cîteaux.[118]

A number of the other topics of the treatise served as direct inspiration for Bernard's contemporaries. Aspects of the discussion of the freedom of man in the face of the loss of free pleasure (11:37-12:40), for instance, were repeated almost word-for-word by Gerhoh of Reichersberg in his *Commentary* on Psalm 31 (c. 1146-47).[119] Other passages influenced the *Commentary* on Psalm 38 written in 1148.[120] Works such as the *Sententia divinitatis* (c. 1145) and the roughly-contemporary *Tractatus de libero arbitrio* of Vivian the Premonstratensian make wide-ranging use of Bernard's work.[121]

Still further, Bernard's strong re-emphasis of the Augustinian tradition, particularly his opposition to Semi-pelagianism under any form, was certainly of real importance, though difficult to trace in its specifically Bernardine form.

The Abbot's contribution to the Scholastic debate on the definition of free choice is capable of more exact determination.[122] Though later Scholastics represented Augustine's

---

116. Controversy still rages over the date and authorship of the work. For the position suggested here, see Lottin, Vol. 1, 25; and J. De Ghellinck, *L'essor de la littérature latine au XIIe siècle* (Paris, 1955), 54-5. On Bernard's influence on the work see also Landgraf, Vol. 1, 88-9; 107; 168.

117. Kleinedam, "De triplicè libertate," 62. Cf. *Libri Sententiarum* II, d. 25.

118. E.g., Adam of Persigny (died 1221), Ep 1 (PL 211:587A).

119. The texts are compared in Faust, 46-7.

120. Leclercq, "Introduction," *Opera,* Vol. 3, 162.

121. Châtillon, 280; and Lottin, Vol. 1, 26-7.

122. The best introduction to the history of the definitions of free choice up to Aquinas may be found in Lottin, Vol. 1, 11-224, especially the summary on 217-24.

view by a definition of freedom of choice as "a faculty of the will and reason,"[123] at the beginning of the Scholastic period the traditional "Augustinian" definition in use was that of "a power of doing good or evil."[124] We have seen Anselm's rejection of this in favor of an essential definition stressing the final cause of freedom—"freedom of choice is the ability to keep uprightness of will for itself alone."[125] Bernard, too, was unsatisfied with the Augustinian definition, but showed his originality by forging his own formula—free choice is a form of consent, i.e., ". . . a spontaneous inclination of the will, or indeed, . . . a self-determining habit of the soul" (2:3). More trenchantly, the Abbot defined it as "freedom from necessity." Some authors have seen an advance in Bernard's definition over that of Anselm, especially in its more adequate treatment of the problem of evil.[126] In any case, Bernard agreed with Anselm more than he differed from him. Liberty defined as freedom from coercion, the complete equation of the voluntary and the free (i.e., that every act of the will as such must be free by definition), and the definition of the soul's justice in terms of its uprightness or "ordination" were all part of the heritage that these two Doctors left to later Scholasticism.[127]

Bernard's definition and its concomitant features became touchstones, frequently cited and commented upon. Hugh of St Victor in his *De sacramentis* (c. 1135-40) also defined free choice through spontaneity, though direct evidence of the

123. William of Auxerre (died 1220) was the first to attribute this definition to Augustine. It actually first is found in Peter Lombard, cf. Lottin, Vol. 1, 64, note 2.

124. This definition was derived from a passage in the *De correptione et gratia*, 1:2: "Liberum itaque arbitrium et ad malum et ad bonum faciendum confitendum est nos habere" (PL 44:917).

125. ". . . libertas arbitrii est potestas servandi rectitudinem voluntatis propter ipsam rectitudinem" *De lib. arbit.* 3 (ed., Vol. 1, 212; translation of J. Hopkins and H. Richardson, *Anselm of Canterbury: Truth, Freedom, and Evil*, N.Y. 1967).

126. Venuta, 164; and Faust, 42-3.

127. On Anselm's influence on Bernard see Gilson, *The Mystical Theology*, 226, note 52.

Abbot's influence is lacking. The *Summa sententiarum*, as might be expected, had a strongly Bernardine doctrine of the relation of will and reason in *liberum arbitrium*.[128] Both Peter Lombard and Richard of St Victor discussed the inadmissability of free choice under the Bernardine rubric of *libertas a necessitate*.[129] In short, the influence of Bernard on his immediate context was extensive.

The Abbot of Clairvaux's importance by no means dwindled in the thirteenth century, for even though theories of the will as an intellectual appetite based on St John Damascene's *De fide orthodoxa* and newly-translated Aristotelian works were becoming increasingly important, the Scholastic mentality always sought to correlate and conciliate its doctrinal authorities. Philip, the Chancellor of the University of Paris (died 1236), was particularly important in popularizing the views of both Anselm and Bernard among later Scholastics.[130] He tried to conciliate the Abbot's claim that free choice was a habit with the enigmatic claim of Peter Lombard that it was a faculty or power;[131] thus creating an unstable position that was bound to be overcome. With two of the most important early masters of the Mendicant orders, the Franciscan Alexander of Hales (died 1245) and the Dominican Albert the Great (active in Paris c. 1243-47), we find that Bernard's definition has become one of four classic positions to be treated in discussing free choice.[132] As the Orders continued to develop and harden their theological traditions during the course of the century, it became obvious that the influence of the Abbot of Clairvaux was more welcome among the Franciscans than among the Dominicans, some-

128. Lottin, Vol. 1, 25-6.
129. Landgraf, Vol. 1, 103.
130. Lottin, 70, note 2.
131. Ibid., 72-6.
132. In Albert the definitions are those of Anselm, Bernard, one attributed to St Peter and the Lombard's version of an "Augustinian" definition (Lottin, 120). With Alexander the four are Anselmian, Bernardine, "Augustine," and philosophical (135-6; 143). This formulation becomes standard in Franciscan authors, e.g., Odo Rigaud (160), and St Bonaventure, *In II Sent.* d. 25, q. 6, 608 (179-80).

thing that held for a dogmatic treatise like the *Grace and Free Choice*, as well as for Bernard's more mystical writings.[133] Although the influence of Bernard was less marked among the Dominicans,[134] it was not totally absent. Scholars have long discussed the nature of the relation of the Abbot's thought to that of Thomas Aquinas, the master of Dominican theology and the *Doctor communis* of the Catholic Church. While avoiding the extreme of attempting to interpret Bernard in the light of Aquinas, as has been done frequently in the past, or of admitting with Châtillon that Aquinas admired Bernard's virtues more than his theology,[135] there still is value in comparing the two, if only to illustrate whatever lines of continuity may have bound together the vast transformation of Western theology in the more than one hundred years between their writings.

The earliest major work of Aquinas, the *Commentary on the Sentences,* displays a great concern with some of the elements of Bernard's thought which had become part of the theological tradition. As already noted, Aquinas defends Bernard's threefold distinction of liberty and even seems influenced by his definition of free choice.[136] In the first part of the *Summa, liberum arbitrium* remains a topic for treatment, and so does the definition;[137] but the latter parts of this work illustrate that Aquinas' mature thought had less and less place for the *liberum arbitrium* on which the Bernardine treatise is based. Does this indicate complete rejection of Bernard's positions? Perhaps not.

Even if Bernard's formulations were sometimes rejected or superceded, this in no way detracts from their significance; it merely shows that like all theological effort they partake of time at least as much as of eternity. The Abbot's definition of free choice was based upon the equation of the free and

133. Châtillon, 281-3.
134. Ibid., 283.
135. Ibid., 284.
136. *In II Sent.* d. 25, q. 1, a. 1, ad 1.
137. Ia, q. 83, a. 2, ad 2.

the voluntary; Thomas Aquinas had evolved a theory of the will in which all actions of the will were voluntary, but not all were free.[138] The distinction of the various historical stages of freedom, while never totally abandoned because of theology's ties to the history of salvation, yielded pride of place in High Scholasticism to the systematic theorem of the supernatural.[139] The Augustinian terms of operative and cooperative grace continued to be used, but took on more technical meanings within the ambit of a systematic theology influenced by a developed theory of the will as an intellectual appetite, the theorem of the supernatural, and a more nuanced understandings of modes of causality.

For all these reasons, Bernard and Thomas may easily be contrasted in many particulars—and not only in the areas mentioned. What is obvious is the dominance of the abstract "predestination-contingency-freedom" schema in the thought of Aquinas.[140] Nevertheless, as G. Venuta has noted well, Bernard's main concern was not the speculative question of how to reconcile grace and free choice; but the dogmatic problem of presenting the Scriptural and ecclesial doctrine of the roles of free choice and grace in the work of salvation.[141] His goal was fundamentally the same as that of Augustine: to penetrate to the heart of Paul's message on grace. His method was also a very similar one—basically that of the comparison, collation, and exegesis of the Scriptural texts. Obscure texts were illuminated by more manifest ones; distinctions (for the most part suggested by the Scriptures themselves) were introduced to handle key problems; pertinent passages were invoked to guide the procedure. Bernard had not been unwilling to go beyond a purely Biblical theology in such areas as working out a definition of free choice; but the purpose behind such forays was always controlled by the overwhelming dogmatic interest of his treatise—that the teaching of the

138. See Lonergan, *Grace and Freedom*, 93-7.

139. Ibid., 18.

140. For one summary of the agreement and difference between the two see the article of Bavaud referred to at the beginning of this Introduction.

141. Venuta, 159.

Church on grace and free choice should shine forth. It is on this level, i.e., insofar as both Bernard and Thomas attempted to be true in their own ways to the fundamental doctrinal tradition of the medieval Church, that we must look for the real agreement between them. Agreement did exist on many important issues: the continuity of some form of freedom after the Fall, coupled with the radical impotence of this freedom to effect a saving act; the absolute prevenience of grace, and the totality of its efficacy; and the admission that through the activity of grace the will can cooperate in the work of its salvation, so that free choice becomes the *locus* of merit. In this sense, at least, the comparison between Bernard and Thomas does show lines of continuity, although their respective visions of the nature of theology and the resources which it should invoke were diverse. Perhaps both Bernard and Aquinas might have thought of this as a case of *diversa sed non adversa*.

One final area of the influence of the *Grace and Free Choice* of the Abbot of Clairvaux deserves mention. It is common knowledge that among medieval authors Bernard stood second to none in the admiration of the Reformers. Given the central position of grace and justification in the theology of the Reformation, the question of the attitude taken by this tradition to the Abbot's treatise is a suggestive one. Since it would be impossible to give an adequate survey of the whole, we will limit ourselves here to a brief evaluation of the attitude of Luther and Calvin toward the *Grace and Free Choice*.

Despite the research that has already been devoted to the topic, the full complexity of Luther's relation to the Abbot of Clairvaux invites further study.[142] It does seem fair to say that after St Augustine, Bernard was Luther's most admired theologian. "I regard him as the most pious of all monks,"

---

142. Among older studies H. Strohl, *L'evolution religieuse de Luther jusqu'en 1515* (Strasbourg, 1922), especially 107-8, might be mentioned. Two recent, but on the whole unsatisfactory, treatments in English are R. Mousnier, "St Bernard and Martin Luther," *American Benedictine Review*, 14 (1963): 448-62; and C. Volz, "Martin Luther's Attitude toward Bernard of Clairvaux," *Studies in Medieval Cistercian History*, CS 13 (Spencer, 1971), 186-204.

said Luther, "and prefer him to all others, even to St Dominic. He is the only one worthy of the name 'Father Bernard' and of being studied diligently."[143] Or again, "St Bernard was a man so lofty in spirit that I almost venture to set him above all other celebrated teachers both ancient and modern."[144] Nevertheless, Luther made it quite clear that there were important limitations to the esteem in which he held the Abbot. Not only the universal principle by which any author was to be followed only insofar as he adhered to the Scriptures,[145] but a more special principle qualified Bernard's position. Luther says: "Bernard was superior to all the Doctors in the Church when he preached, but he became quite a different man in his disputations, for then he attributed too much to law and to free will."[146] It seems obvious, then, that Luther thought that there was an essential difference between Bernard the preacher and Bernard the dogmatician, and that his admiration for the former did not extend to the latter.[147] The reason for this is not hard to see. While Luther always praised Bernard's emphasis on personal faith in Christ as essential for justification,[148] there were many aspects of the Abbot's teaching on grace and free choice which could

---

143. *Sermons on the Gospel of John, 33*, in *Luther's Works. American Edition*, Vol. 22:388 (hereafter referred to as AE).

144. *To the Councilmen of Germany* (AE 45:363). For other statements of Luther lauding Bernard see Mousnier, 450.

145. Texts to illustrate the application of this principle to Bernard will be found in Volz, 194-5, and 200-1.

146. *Table Talk* #584 (AE 54:105). Similar remarks may be found in the *Commentary on Psalm 117* (AE 14:38); and *Table Talk* #5439a (not translated in AE, but can be found in the critical edition of Luther's works, the *Weimerer Ausgabe, Tischreden*, Vol. 5, 154). This text contains an explicit reference to the *Grace and Free Choice*: "For Bernard, nothing is worthwhile but Jesus; in his debates, for example the one about free will, Jesus is nowhere to be found." One is permitted to wonder if Luther really knew the treatise well, or if he was merely using his customary exaggeration.

147. Mousnier, 451-2.

148. W. Pauck, "General Introduction," *Luther: Lectures on Romans* (Library of Christian Classics, Philadelphia, 1961), p. I. One example taken from these *Lectures* would be the commentary on 8:16-8, which quotes Bernard's *First Sermon on the Annunciation* (OB 5:234); further texts are collected in Volz, 188-9; 198.

scarcely have been to his liking. The Reformer's great work, *On the Bondage of the Will*, penned in response to the challenge of Erasmus, makes this clear. H. McSorley has pointed out that the fact that Luther rejected freedom of choice in this work did not mean a complete denial of liberty to fallen man;[149] but it cannot be denied that Luther's views on the relation of grace and the human will would naturally have led him to take a jaundiced view of a number of the tenets of the *Grace and Free Choice*, such as its doctrine of good works and merits, and its defense of the permanence of free choice in fallen man.[150] Though Luther's major difficulties with traditional orthodox (i.e. non-Semi-pelagian) formulae may come from his denial of the two kinds of necessity which medieval authors utilized to solve the problems of what we have called the abstract complex,[151] even on the level of the concrete complex of "sin-grace-freedom" the distance between him and Bernard is a real one.

Nonetheless, this should not blind us to the areas of doctrinal agreement that do not exist, particularly those on the impotence of fallen man and the prevenience and efficacy of grace which both authors inherited from Augustine.[152] There are also some texts where Luther's explicit denials may mask at least partial agreement.[153] Of course, Luther's dis-

---

149. *Luther,* 246-50; 256-60; 310-13; 369. Luther's denial of freedom of choice is directed against the definition of Erasmus that is based upon the un-Bernardine liberty of indifference. This is why we can assert that although things happen necessarily they do not happen compulsorily. See *On the Bondage of the Will* (*Library of Christian Classics*, Vol 17, 139-41).

150. Many Catholic authors, e.g., Stutz, 50-1; and Gilson, *The Mystical Theology,* 223-4, note 33, have been quick to point out the differences.

151. Even here McSorley attempts to show that Luther's explicit denial involved an implicit acceptance (315-20).

152. In earlier works, particularly the *Lectures on Romans,* Luther may have been at times basing himself directly on the *De gratia et libero arbitrio,* e.g., his remarks about conformity to the Word (6:16-7, trans. Pauck, 188) may be dependent on Gra 10:33.

153. E.g., in denying the cooperation of the will in the work of man's recreation (*On the Bondage of the Will,* Library of Christian Classics trans., 289), Luther obviously distances himself from Bernard (Gra 14:46). Luther does, however, admit some kind of cooperation even in this passage: "But he [God] does not work in us without us, because it is for this very thing that he has recreated and preserves us, that he might work in us and we might cooperate with him." In

tinction between Bernard the preacher and Bernard the disputant is a false one—there is no essential difference in the positions the Abbot held in the two kinds of works.[154] But what led the reformer to make the differentiation? Was it a question of selective acquaintance, unconscious mental censorship,[155] or what? Again, the anomalies await further investigation.

The relation of Bernard's treatise to John Calvin's theology is less ambiguous than its connection with Luther.[156] Calvin's penchant for scholarship and his precision have much to account for this. Nevertheless, we are still lacking a satisfactory evaluation of all the substantive issues. Forty-seven passages from the Abbot's writings are cited in Calvin's *Institutes of the Christian Religion*;[157] and his extensive knowledge of the treatise on *Grace and Free Choice* is amply illustrated. Insofar as direct citations from the treatise are involved, Calvin mentions Bernard's definition of free will in his discussion of the question (*Institutes* 2, 2, 4), though he apparently holds it lacking due to its obscurity. The Geneva reformer's reaction to Bernard's three states of freedom seems to be conditioned by his knowledge of the history of the distinction in Scholastic theology. In 2, 2, 5, he accepts the distinction ". . . except in so far as necessary is falsely confused with compulsion;"[158] while in 2, 3, 5 he apparently holds that Bernard himself did not fall into this pitfall while Peter Lombard did.[159] He might well have added that many of the Scholastics who made use of the distinction also affirmed a

Bernard's categories of "thinking, willing, and accomplishing," it seems that Luther would admit cooperation in the case of the third, but not in the case of the second.

154. As pointed out by Mousnier, 458-9.

155. Ibid., 460.

156. E.g., See Bavaud for a general survey.

157. See Index II under "Bernard of Clairvaux" in *Institutes of the Christian Religion*, translated by F. Battles and edited by J. McNeill (Library of Christian Classics, Vols. 20-1, Philadelphia, 1960), Vol. 2, 1601.

158. Ibid., Vol. 1, 262.

159. The passage praises Bernard's Augustinian dictum (Gra 6:16) that free choice makes us willers and grace willers of the good. It includes a lengthy quotation from SC 81:7. This dictum of the Abbot is again commended in 2, 5, 14; and the SC passage is also cited in 2, 5, 1.

difference between necessity and compulsion. Calvin, however, also criticizes some positions Bernard had adopted in the *Grace and Free Choice.* In 1, 15, 3, he rejects any doctrine of man as the image of God which makes use of the un-Biblical attempt to distinguish between image and likeness; while in 2, 2, 6, he explicitly condemns Bernard's doctrine of operating and cooperating grace.[160] All in all, though, Calvin's attitude towards Bernard is a remarkably positive one. In 2, 3, 12, he praises his understanding of the prevenient character of grace,[161] and in 3, 11, 22 couples Bernard with Augustine in recognizing that men are made righteous by the free acceptance of God. Most interestingly, in 3, 12, 2, Calvin even seems willing to accept the doctrine of merit that he found in the Abbot of Clairvaux. As we have seen at the end of *Grace and Free Choice,* man's fundamental ground for confidence is not in his own merits but in the promise by which God has freely bound himself, a promise made visible in Jesus' Christ.[162] Calvin is willing to concentrate on this aspect of Bernard's teaching and excuse others—"the fact that he uses the term 'merits' freely for good works, we must excuse as the custom of the time."[163]

Thus we can see that Bernard's *Grace and Free Choice,* the most mature dogmatic product of his pen, did not lose its influence in the new theological world of the Reformation.

160. There seems to be some confusion about what text of Bernard that Calvin may have had in mind here, since the Abbot speaks of operating and cooperating grace in Gra 14:47 and not 14:46, as the editors of the *Library of Christian Classics* suggest. The point that Calvin is making against Bernard does not, however, apply to 14:47. Calvin says: "Thus Bernard declares the good will is God's work, yet concedes to man that of his own impluse he seeks this sort of good will" (ed., Vol. 1, 263); but for Bernard the good counsel which seeks the good will is always sown by divine activity. The Abbot does, of course, differ from the reformer insofar as he could be included under the latter's second heading of false views on the nature of cooperating grace, those who think that we " . . . confirm it by obediently following it."

161. Citing SC 21:9.

162. The texts that Calvin refers to here are not from Gra 14:51, but from *In Qui inhabit* 15:5; and SC 13:4; 61:3; 68:6. The basic doctrine does not differ, however, though the Christological dimension is stronger in the passages cited.

163. *Institutes,* ed. McNeill, 758. Other passages in which Calvin praises Bernard's understanding of merits are 3, 12, 8 (using SC 13:5); and 3, 15, 2 (citing SC 68:6).

Just as in the Scholastic context, it was widely read, sometimes followed as authoritative and sometimes criticized. Like all great works of theology, *Grace and Free Choice* is at once intensely time-bound—the product of one man working in the light of a certain dogmatic tradition with a limited number of resources at his disposal—and yet in some way perhaps timeless. The timelessness of theological masterpieces is itself a theological question of no small dimension. Reading Bernard may not provide answers to current theological problems, but it may enable the modern reader to experience something of the elusive transcendence of all true theological classics.

Bernard McGinn

The University of Chicago

PROLOGUE

WITH GOD'S HELP, in so far as I could, I have brought to a conclusion this work on grace and free choice which I recently began on an occasion know to you.[1] I fear nevertheless that I may be found to have spoken less worthily than I might have of these great matters, or to have repeated unnecessarily what has already been treated of by others.[2] You please read it first, therefore, and if you think best, privately; lest, if it be read for the first time in public, it may perhaps advertise the author's temerity more than edify the reader's charity. Then, should you judge it useful to be read publicly, if you notice something obscurely stated which, in an obscure subject, might yet have been more clearly expressed, without departing from due brevity, do not hesitate either to amend it yourself or else to return it to me for emendation, unless you wish to be deprived of that promise of Wisdom where it says: "Those who explain me will have life everlasting."[3]

1. In the Latin the second person plural is employed throughout the Prologue.
2. For example, St Augustine, Prosper of Acquitaine, Hilary of Arles and Faustus of Riez, Fathers of the Second Council of Orange (AD 529), and St Anselm.
3. Sir 24:31 (Vulgate).

CHAPTER ONE

FOR THE MERIT OF A GOOD WORK THERE IS NEEDED, ALONG WITH THE GRACE OF GOD, THE CONSENT OF FREE CHOICE.[1]

ONCE, IN CONVERSATION, I happened to refer to my experience of God's grace, how I recognized myself as being impelled to good by its prevenient action, felt myself being borne along by it, and helped, with its help, to find perfection. "What part do *you* play, then," asked a bystander, "or what reward or prize do you hope for, if it is all God's work? " "What do you think yourself? " I replied. "Glorify God,"[2] said he, "who freely went before you, aroused and set you moving; and then live a worthy life to prove your gratitude for kindnesses received and your suitability for receiving more." "That is sound advice," I observed, "if only you could give me the means to carry it out. Indeed, it is easier to know what one ought to do than to do it; for it is one thing to lead the blind and another thing to provide a vehicle for the weary. Not every guide supplies the traveller with the food for the journey. The one who sets him in the right direction gives him one thing, the one who provides him with food to keep him from fainting on the way, another.[3] So, too, not every teacher is automatically a communicator of the good he teaches. Hence, I stand in need of two things: instruction and help. You, man, certainly give fine instruction to my ignorance; but, unless the Apostle be

1. The chap. titles are adopted, with some slight modifications, from Watkin Williams, tr. (London: SPCK, 1920), as these seem clear and helpful. They are derived from Mabillon.
2. Jn 9:24.
3. Mt 15:32.

mistaken, the Spirit helps our weakness.[4] Indeed, the One who advises me by means of your words, must assist me also through his Spirit, so that I may be able to do as you advise. For it already is due partly to this assistance that I can will what is right, but I cannot do it;[5] but I would have no grounds for believing that I would some day manage to do it, were it not that he who has given me to will, shall also enable me to accomplish on account of my good will."[6] — "Where, then," said he, "are our merits, or where our hope? " — "Listen," I replied, "He saved us, not because of deeds done by us in righteousness, but in virtue of his own mercy. [7] What? Did you imagine that you create your own merits,[8] that you can be saved by your own righteousness, who cannot even say 'Jesus is Lord' without the Holy Spirit? [9] Or have you forgotten the words: 'Without me you can do nothing,'[10] and, 'It depends not upon man's will or exertion, but upon God's mercy'? "[11]

2. Maybe you are saying: "What part, then, does free choice play? " I shall answer you in one word: it is saved. Take away free choice and there is nothing to be saved. Take away grace and there is no means of saving. Without the two combined, this work cannot be done: the one as operative principle, the other as object toward which, or in which, it is accomplished. God is the author of salvation, the free willing faculty merely capable of receiving it. None but God can give it, nothing but free choice receive it. What, therefore, is given by God alone and to free choice alone, can no more happen without the recipient's consent than without the bestower's grace. Consequently, free choice is said to co-operate with operating grace in its act of consent, or, in other words, in its

4. Rom 8:26.
5. Rom 7:18.
6. See Phil 2:13.
7. Tit 3:5.
8. Cf. chapter 13 below; also SC 68:6, OB 2:200.
9. 1 Cor 12:3.
10. Jn 15:5.
11. Rom 9:16.

process of being saved.[12] For, to consent is to be saved. That is why the animal spirit does not receive this salvation: it lacks the power of voluntary consent, by which it might tranquilly submit to a saving God, whether by acquiescing in his commands, or by believing his promises, or by giving thanks for his benefits.

VOLUNTARY CONSENT IS ONE THING, NATURAL APPETITE ANOTHER [13]

For voluntary consent is one thing, natural appetite another. The latter we hold in common with irrational animals.[14] Ensnared by the allurements of the flesh, it has not the power of giving consent to the spirit.[15] Perhaps it is this the Apostle is referring to under another name as "the wisdom of the flesh," when he says: "The wisdom of the flesh is hostile to God; it does not submit to God's law, indeed it cannot."[16] It is voluntary consent, as I say, that distinguishes us from this last which we share with the animals.

DEFINITION OF VOLUNTARY CONSENT

For voluntary consent is a self-determining habit of the soul. Its action is neither forced nor extorted. It stems from the will and not from necessity, denying or giving itself on no issue except by way of the will. But if it is compelled in spite of itself, then there is violent, not voluntary, consent. Where

12. The terms *salus* and *salvari* have the technical meaning here of "wholeness" in the Christian sense, and "being made whole." Cf., for example, Acts 2:47 and 2 Cor 6:2. This will recur as the treatise develops. On the contemporary importance of this, and of the thought underlying it, see A. Forest's essay "S. Bernard et notre temps" in *S. Bernard Theologien*, ASOC 9 (1953) (Rome: Editiones Cistercienses, 1954), 294f.

13. The subtitles, 47 in number, are found in uniform style in at least 15 mss., including some of the most ancient, from all different regions. They have been retained in the critical edition as they are found in Dijon 658, and have been translated here, thus showing the text as it was commonly seen even in Bernard's time. See Leclercq's Introduction, OB 3:158-163.

14. On the place of this *naturalis appetitus* in Bernard's degrees of love, see P. Delfgaauw's essay in the work just cited, pp. 234-252, especially p. 238.

15. See Gal 5:17.

16. Rom 8:7.

the will is absent, so is consent; for only what is voluntary may be called consent. Hence, where you have consent, there also is the will. But where the will is, there is freedom. And this is what I understand by the term "free choice."

CHAPTER TWO

IN WHAT FREE CHOICE CONSISTS

FOR GREATER CLARITY, HOWEVER, and in order to be better equipped for what lies ahead, perhaps we should examine this somewhat more deeply. In the material world, life is not identical with sense-perception, not sense-perception with appetite; nor appetite with consent. This should become more evident from the definitions of each. For life in any body is an internal and natural movement, having existence only within the confines of that body.

DEFINITION OF SENSE

Whereas sense-perception is a vital movement in the body, alert and outward,

DEFINITION OF NATURAL APPETITE

And natural appetite, a force in a living being, intent on getting the senses moving,

DEFINITION OF CONSENT

Consent, on the other hand, is a spontaneous inclination of the will, or indeed, as I recall expressing it earlier, a self-determining habit of the soul.

DEFINITION OF WILL

Will is a rational movement, governing both sense-perception and appetite. In whatever direction it turns, it has reason as its mate, one might even say as its follower. Not that it is moved invariably by reason —indeed it does many things through reason against reason, or, in other words, through the medium of reason as it were, yet contrary to its counsel and judgment—but it is never moved without reason. Hence it is said: "The sons of this world are more prudent in their own generation than the sons of light";[1] and again, "They are wise in doing evil."[2] Indeed, prudence or wisdom cannot be present in a creature, even in wrongdoing, by any means other than by reason.

4. Reason is given to the will for instruction, not destruction. It would be to the destruction of the will, however, were it to impose any necessity on it which would prevent it from moving freely in accordance with its judgment. Such necessity might push it (consenting to appetite or evil spirit) toward wrong, making an animal of it, not knowing, or even actively resisting the things which are of the Spirit of God; or (following grace) toward right, making it spiritual, able to judge all things, but itself judged by no one.[3] If, I say, the will were incapable of reaching out to any of these because of some prohibition of the reason, it would no longer be will. For, the presence of necessity means the absence of will.

WITHOUT THE CONSENT OF ITS OWN WILL THE RATIONAL CREATURE CAN NOT BE MADE JUST OR UNJUST

If the rational creature would, out of necessity and without the consent of its own will, be made just or unjust, it ought on no account to be dejected, nor could it possibly be elated, since in either case that one faculty would be lacking which is

1. Lk 16:8.
2. Jer 4:22.
3. 1 Cor 2:14f.

capable in it of happiness or unhappiness, namely the will. Those other things listed above: life, sense-perception, and appetite, of themselves make one neither happy nor unhappy. Were this not so, trees because of their life, and animals because of the other two, would be subject to sorrow or worthy of beatitude; but this is out of the question. We have life in common with the trees, and sense-perception, appetite, and again, life with the animals; it is then what we call the will which distinguishes us from both of them. The consent of this will, voluntary, of course, and not necessary, proves us to be just or unjust, and also, meritedly, makes us happy or miserable. Such consent, on account of the imperishable freedom of the will and the inevitable judgment of the reason always and everywhere accompanying it, is, I think, well called free choice, having free disposal of itself because of the will and the power to judge of itself because of the reason. It is only right that judgment should accompany freedom, as whatever has the free disposal of itself, should it chance to sin, judges itself in the act of sinning. And it really is judgment, because if he sins, he suffers justly indeed, what he does not will, who does not sin unless he wills.

5. On what basis, in fact, can one impute anything to a man, whether good or bad, if he is not known to have the free disposal of himself? Necessity excuses from both. For necessity's presence means freedom's absence; and where there is no freedom, neither is there merit, nor consequently judgment, apart from the case of original sin, for that, clearly, is another matter. Moreover, whatever lacks this freedom of voluntary consent, lacks also undoubtedly merit and judgment. Hence, everything pertaining to man, will alone excepted, is free from both alike, since it has not the free disposal of itself. Thus life, sense-perception, appetite, memory, temperament, and the like, are subject to necessity to the extent that they are not fully subject to the will. But as to the will, since it is impossible for it not to obey itself—no one does not will what he wills, or wills what he does not will—so is it impossible for it to be deprived of its freedom.

AN ACT OF THE WILL CANNOT BE CHANGED EXCEPT
INTO ANOTHER ACT OF THE WILL

An act of the will can, indeed, be changed, but only into another act of the will, so that freedom is never lost. The will can thus no more be deprived of it than of itself. Should it ever happen to be in man's power to will nothing at all, or to will something but not by his willing faculty, then the will would be capable of lacking freedom. That is why we impute nothing they do, whether good or ill, to the mentally deficient, to infants, to the sleeping, because, even as they are no longer masters of their reason, so neither do they retain the use of their own will, nor consequently the judgment of freedom. Since, therefore, the will knows no freedom other than itself, it is right that its judgment should arise only out of itself. For never do dullness of wit, weakness of memory, restlessness of appetite, obtuseness of sense-perception, nor slackening of vitality of themselves constitute a person guilty, even as their contraries do not make him innocent; and this for no other reason than that all these are known to occur necessarily at times, and without previous consultation of the will.

CHAPTER THREE

A THREEFOLD FREEDOM: OF NATURE, OF GRACE, AND OF GLORY [1]

ONLY THE WILL, THEN, since, by reason of its innate freedom, it can be compelled by no force or necessity to dissent from itself, or to consent in any matter in spite of itself, makes a creature righteous or unrighteous, capable and deserving of happiness or of sorrow, insofar as it shall have consented to righteousness or unrighteousness. That is why we defined earlier on, —and not unsuitably I think, — such voluntary and free consent, on which every act of judgment, as we have seen, depends, as "free choice"; "free" referring to the will, "choice" to the reason. But free though it is, this does not signify the freedom of which the Apostle says: "Where the Spirit of the Lord is, there is freedom."[2]

FREEDOM FROM SIN

For here he means freedom from sin, as he points out elsewhere: "When you were slaves of sin, you were free in regard to righteousness. But now that you have been set free from sin and have become slaves of God, the return you get is sanctification and its end, eternal life."[3] Who in sinful flesh[4]

1. In his doctoral thesis, *Libero Arbitrio e Libertà della Grazia nel Pensiero di S. Bernardo*, (Rome: Ferrari, 1953), p. 17, Dom G. Venuta S O CIST. rightly observes that Bernard's teaching on freedom is an essential part of his mystical doctrine, and that both are a function of his monastic ideal.
2. 2 Cor 3:17.
3. Rom 6:20, 22.
4. Rom 8:3.

would claim to be free from sin? So I certainly do not believe that free choice takes its name from this type of freedom.

FREEDOM FROM SORROW

There is also a freedom from sorrow, of which the Apostle again says: "The creation itself will be set free from its bondage to decay and obtain the glorious liberty of the children of God."[5] But would anyone in this mortal condition dare arrogate to himself even this kind of freedom? Hence, we deny also that free choice takes its name from this freedom.

FREEDOM FROM NECESSITY

There is, however, a freedom which seems to me to fit it better, and which we might designate freedom fron necessity, since "necessary" appears to be contrary to "voluntary." What is done by necessity does not derive from the will, and vice versa.

A THREEFOLD FREEDOM

7. There are, then, these three forms of freedom, as they have occured to us: freedom from sin, from sorrow and from necessity. The last belongs to our natural condition; to the first we are restored by grace; and the second is reserved for us in our homeland.

THERE ARE SAID TO BE THREE LIBERTIES: THE FIRST, OF NATURE; THE SECOND, OF GRACE; THE THIRD, OF LIFE OR GLORY.

The first freedom, therefore, might be termed freedom of nature, the second of grace, the third of life or glory. For in the first place, we were created with free will and willing freedom, a creature noble in God's eyes. Secondly, we are re-formed in innocence, a new creature in Christ:[6] and

5. Rom 8:21.
6. 2 Cor 5:17; Gal 6:15.

thirdly, we are raised up to glory, a perfect creature in the Spirit. The first freedom is thus a title of considerable honor; the second, of even greater power; and the last, of total happiness. By the first, we have the advantage over other living things; by the second, over the flesh; while by the third, we cast down death itself.[7] Or, to express it another way, just as in the first, God put under our feet sheep and oxen and the beasts of the field,[8] so did he likewise, in the second, crush and lay low beneath our feet those spiritual beasts of the world of whom it is said: "Do not deliver the souls of those who trust in you to the wild beasts."[9] Finally, by the last-named, in our own more perfect submission to ourselves through victory over corruption and death—when, that is, death shall be last of all destroyed[10]—we will pass over into the glorious freedom of the sons of God,[11] the freedom by which Christ will set us free, when he delivers us as a kingdom to God the Father.[12] Of this, I think, and also of the one we have called freedom from sin, he said to the Jews: "If the Son makes you free, you will be free indeed."[13] He meant that even free choice stands in need of a liberator, but one, of course, who would set it free, not from necessity which was quite unknown to it since this pertains to the will, but rather from sin, into which it had fallen both freely and willingly, and also from the penalty of sin which it carelessly incurred and has unwillingly borne. From these two evils it was quite unable to extricate itself, except through him who alone of all men was made free among the dead;[14] free, that is, from sin in the midst of sinners.

8. He alone, indeed, among the sons of Adam was free from sin, he "who committed no sin; nor was there any guile found on his lips,"[15] he also possessed freedom from sorrow

7. See 1 Cor 15:26.
8. See Ps 8:8.
9. Ps 74:19.
10. 1 Cor 15:26.
11. Rom 8:21.
12. See 1 Cor 15:24.
13. Jn 8:36.
14. Ps 88:5 (Vg).
15. 1 Pet 2:22.

which is the penalty of sin, but this he possessed only in potency, not in act. Thus no one took away his life from him, but he laid it down of his own accord.[16] In a word, as the Prophet had foretold, "He was offered up because he willed it,"[17] and even as, at the time of his own choosing, he was "born of woman, born under the law, to redeem those who were under the law."[18] Hence, he, too, was subject to the law of suffering; but this was because he willed to be, in order that, himself free among sufferers and sinners, he might lift from his brothers' shoulders the yoke of both sin and suffering.

THE SAVIOR HAD THESE THREE LIBERTIES

He, therefore, enjoyed all three freedoms: the first by his human and divine nature combined, the others by his divine power. As to whether or not the first man was endowed with the last two in paradise, or how or to what extent he had them—of this, more presently.

16. Jn 10:18.
17. Isa 53:7 (Vg).
18. Gal 4:4f.

CHAPTER FOUR

WHAT KIND OF FREEDOM BELONGS TO THE HOLY SOULS IN THEIR
DISEMBODIED STATE WHAT KIND BELONGS TO GOD AND WHAT
KIND IS COMMON TO ALL RATIONAL CREATURES

THIS MUCH IS CERTAIN: that both these freedoms, from sin and suffering, are fully and perfectly present in those perfect souls who have been loosed from fleshly bonds, even as they are in God and his Christ, and the angels in heaven. For though the souls of the just, while they have not yet received their bodies, lack undoubtedly some measure of glory, they experience no trace of sorrow.

FREEDOM FROM NECESSITY IS IN BOTH GOOD
AND EVIL RATIONAL CREATURES

Freedom from necessity belongs alike to God and to every rational creature, good or bad. Neither by sin nor by suffering is it lost or lessened; nor is it greater in the just man than in the sinner, nor fuller in the angel than in man. For the consent of the human will, which is directed by grace toward the good, makes man freely good, and, in the good, free, by the fact that it is voluntarily given and not unwillingly dragged out. In the same way, when it inclines willingly toward the bad, it makes man nonetheless free and spontaneous in the bad. He is not forced to be evil by some other cause, but simply chooses to be so at the behest of his own will. And just as the angels in heaven, or even God himself, remain freely good, that is, by their own will, not from any extrinsic necessity; so the devil freely both opted for evil and persists in it, not by coercion from without, but of his own free choice. Freedom of will thus continues to exist, even where the mind is captive, as full in the bad as in the good, yet more orderly in the good; and as complete in its own way in the creature as in the Creator, yet more powerfully in the Creator.[1]

10. When a person complains and says: "I *wish* I could have a good will, but I just can't manage it," this in no way argues against the freedom of which we have been speaking, as if the will thus suffered violence or were subject to necessity. Rather is he witnessing to the fact that he lacks that freedom which is called freedom from sin. Because, whoever wants to have a good will proves thereby that he has a will, since his desire is aimed at good only through his will. And if he finds himself unable to have a good will whereas he really wants to, then this is because he feels freedom is lacking to him, freedom namely from sin, by which it pains him that his will is oppressed, though not suppressed.[2] Indeed it is more than likely that, since he wants to have a good will, he does, in fact, to some extent, have it. What he wants is good, and he could hardly want good otherwise than by means of good will; just as he could want evil only by a bad will. When we desire good, then our will is good; when evil, evil. In either case, there is will; and everywhere freedom; necessity yields to will. But if we are unable to do what we will, we feel that freedom itself is somehow captive to sin, or that it is unhappy, not that it is lost.

11. In my opinion, therefore, free choice takes its name from that freedom alone by which the will is free either to judge itself good if it has consented to good, or bad, if to evil; only by willing, in fact, can it feel itself to consent to either. For freedom from sin might, perhaps, more fittingly be called free counsel; and freedom from sorrow, free pleasure, rather than free choice.

---

1. E. Gilson compares this passage with Descartes teaching on liberty, *La Liberté chez Descartes et la théologie,* (Paris: Alcan, 1913), pp. 230-243.

2. "Premi non perimi." W. W. Williams observes, "The *jeu de mots* is singularly happy, but difficult to render in English. 'Suppress' is strong enough, if we remember the original sense of *supprimo,* to sink a ship to the bottom of the sea." *The Treatise of St Bernard Concerning Grace and Free Will,* (London: Society for Promoting Christian Knowlege, 1920), p. 19, note 2.

JUDGMENT, COUNSEL, AND PLEASURE

Choice is an act of judgment. But even as it belongs to judgment to distinguish between what is lawful and what not, so it belongs to counsel to examine what is expedient and what not, and to pleasure, to experience what is pleasant and what not. If only we took counsel for our profit as freely as we judge our deeds! so that, as we freely distinguish by our judgment between right and wrong, we might also, by counsel, choose the licit as more suitable and reject the illicit as harmful. Then we would not only be free in our choice, but undoubtedly also free in counsel, and consequently, free from sin. But, supposing all and only that which was expedient or lawful gained our assent? Might we not in this case be also regarded as free with respect to pleasure, feeling as we do that we are free from everything that could displease, in other words from every sorrow? Now, however, since we discern many things by means of the judgment as either to be done or omitted, which we nevertheless choose or reject through counsel in a manner quite at variance with the rectitude of our judgment; and since, again, we do not freely embrace as pleasing all that we observe with counsel as being right and suitable, but impatiently endure it, rather, as something hard and burdensome; it is evident that we possess neither free counsel nor free pleasure.

12. Another question concerns whether Adam possessed these prior to sin. This we shall discuss in due course. But one thing is certain: we *shall* possess them when, by God's mercy, we shall obtain what we pray for: "Thy will be done, on earth as it is in heaven."[3] This shall come to pass when that which appears, as has been said, common to every rational creature, namely, a choice which is free from necessity, shall be in the elect of the human race also—as it is already in the holy angels—secure from sin and safe from sorrow, the happy experience of that threefold liberty proving what is the will of God, good, acceptable and perfect.[4] In the meantime, this

3. Mt 6:10.
4. See Rom 12:2.

is not yet so; in its full measure, men have only freedom of choice. Freedom of counsel they possess merely in part, —that is, the few spiritual ones among them, who have crucified their flesh with its passions and desires,[5] so that sin no longer reigns in their mortal body.[6] Now, it is freedom of counsel which brings it about that sin does not so reign. That it still has some small hold is due to the fact of free choice's still being captive. "But when the perfect comes, then the imperfect will pass away."[7] This means: when freedom of counsel shall have been fully achieved, the judgment's shackles shall also fall away. And that is what we daily ask in prayer, when we say to God: "Thy kingdom come."[8] This kingdom is not yet wholly established among us. But it comes closer by degrees each day, and, daily more and more it gradually extends its bounds. It does so in those only whose interior self, with the help of God, is renewed from day to day.[9] In the measure, therefore, that grace's kingdom is extended, sin's power is weakend. It is a process which is still unfinished because of this perishable body which weighs down the soul[10] and because of the needy condition of this earthly dwelling[11] which burdens the mind full of thoughts.[12] Even those who appear more perfect in this mortal state have to acknowledge that "In many things we all offend"[13] and "if we say we have no sin, we deceive ourselves, and the truth is not in us."[14] That is why they pray without ceasing:[15] "Thy kingdom come."[16] But this will not be accomplished even in them until not only has sin no further sway over their perishable body,[17] but also there neither is nor can be any sin at all in the body, then immortal.

5. See Gal 5:24.
6. See Rom 6:12.
7. See 1 Cor 13:10.
8. Mt 6:10.
9. See 2 Cor 4:16.
10. See Wis 9:15; Rom 7:24.
11. See Wis 9:15; 2 Cor 5:1; 2 Pet 1:13.
12. See Wis 9:15.
13. Jas 3:2.
14. 1 Jn 1:8.
15. See 1 Thess 5:17.
16. Mt 6:10.
17. See Rom 6:12.

CHAPTER FIVE

WHETHER FREEDOM FROM SORROW OR FREEDOM
OF COUNSEL IS GRANTED IN THIS WORLD

WHAT NOW SHALL WE SAY about freedom of
pleasure in this present evil age[1] where the day's
own trouble is scarcely sufficient for the day,[2] where
every creature groans and is in labor until now, subjected as it
is to futility not of its own will,[3] where the life of man is a
hard service upon the earth,[4] where even the spiritual, who
have already received the first fruits of the Spirit, groan inwardly, awaiting the redemption of their body?[5] Can there
really be room in such a situation for this type of freedom?
What is left free for our good pleasure, I ask, where every
square inch seems taken up by sorrow? Indeed, here not
even innocence or righteousness are immune to sorrow (any
more than they are to sin), where the just man cries out:
"Wretched man that I am! Who will deliver me from this
body of death?"[6] And again: "My tears have been my food
day and night."[7] Where night follows day and day night in
one rhythm of sorrow, there is no moment's room for real
pleasure. Lastly, all who desire to live a godly life in Christ
will suffer persecution[8] most of all, since judgment begins
with the household of God,[9] as he commanded, saying:
"Begin at my sanctuary."[10]

1. See Gal 1:4.
2. See Mt 6:34.
3. See Rom 8:20-22.
4. See Job 7:1.
5. See Rom 8:23.

6. Rom 7:24.
7. Ps 42:3.
8. See 2 Tim 3:12.
9. See 1 Pet 4:17.
10. Ezek 9:6.

14. Yet, though virtue is not immune, perhaps vice is; and at times, at rest from sorrow, feels the touch of pleasure? No, indeed. For those who rejoice in doing evil, and delight in the worst sort of things,[11] imitate the wild laughter of the mad. For no sorrow is more truly sorrow than false joy. And the more in this a thing wears the guise of happiness, the more actually is it misery. As the Wise Man says: "It is better to go to the house of mourning than to go to the house of feasting."[12]

CORPORAL JOY IS NOT WITHOUT SORROW

A certain pleasure is to be found in goods of the body, namely in eating, drinking, warm clothing, and in other such nutriments or coverings of the flesh. But do even these, in fact, escape from sorrow? Bread is fine, but to one who is hungry; drink delightful, but to the thirsty. To the sated, food and drink are a burden, not a joy. Once hunger has been eased, bread will mean little to you; thirst slaked, even the most limpid stream will no more attract you than a swamp. Only those who are hot seek the shade; only the cold or those in darkness hail the sun. None of these things pleases without the prick of necessity. Take this away, and at once the pleasure itself which seemed to form part of them yields to tedium and distate.

A CONCLUSION

It must therefore be admitted here, again, that everything belonging to the present life involves suffering. The only mitigating factor is that, in the relentless hardships which go with our more difficult undertakings, lighter tasks come as a sort of relaxation. In a given time and situation, while heavy and light alternate, the experience of the light seems to provide an interlude to sorrow, as when sometimes we think it a joy when we pass out of the doldrums of nerve-racking trials into worries of a milder kind.

---

11. See Prov 2:14.   12. Eccles 7:2.

THOSE TAKEN UP IN CONTEMPLATION ENJOY
THE FREEDOM OF PLEASURE

15. But what of those who, at times, being caught up in the Spirit through excess of contemplation, become capable of savoring something of the sweetness of heavenly bliss? Do these attain to freedom from sorrow as often as this happens to them? Yes, indeed. Even in this present life, those who with Mary have chosen the better part, which shall not be taken away from them,[13] enjoy freedom of pleasure; rarely, however, and fleetingly. This is undeniable. For those who now possess that which shall never be taken away, plainly experience what is to come: in a word, happiness. And since happiness and sorrow are incompatible, through the Spirit they participate in the former, as often as they cease to feel the latter. Hence, on this earth, contemplatives alone can in some way enjoy freedom of pleasure, though only in part,[14] in very small part, and on the rarest occasions.

THE JUST IN NO SMALL PART ENJOY FREEDOM OF COUNSEL

As to freedom of counsel: every righteous man enjoys it, in part again, but in no small part.

FREEDOM OF CHOICE

Furthermore, as was evident in what we said earlier, freedom of choice belongs to everyone who has the use of reason; no less, essentially, to the bad than to the good; as fully in this life as in the next.

---

13. See Lk 10:42.　　　14. See 1 Cor 13:9-12.

CHAPTER SIX

GRACE IS NECESSARY IN ORDER THAT WE MAY WILL WHAT IS GOOD

I THINK IT HAS BEEN CLEARLY SHOWN that even freedom of choice is to some extent held captive as long as it is unaccompanied or imperfectly accompanied by the two remaining freedoms; and that from no other cause arises this frailty of ours of which the Apostle speaks: "So that you do not the things you would."[1] To will lies in our power indeed as a result of free choice, but not to carry out what we will. I am not saying to will the good or to will the bad, but simply to will. For to will the good indicates an achievement; and to will the bad, a defect; whereas simply to will denotes the subject itself which does either the achieving or the failing. To this subject, however, creating grace gives existence. Saving grace gives it the achievement. But when it fails, it is to blame for its own failure. Free choice, accordingly, constitutes us willers; grace, willers of the good. Because of our willing faculty, we are able to will; but because of grace, to will the good. Just as, simply to fear is one thing, and to fear God, another; to love, one, and to love God, another, —since to fear and to love, on their own. signify affections, but, coupled with the additional word "God," virtues, —so also will is one thing, and to will the good, another.

17. For mere affections live naturally in us, as of us, but those additional acts, as of grace. This means only that grace sets in order what creation has given, so that virtues are no-

1. See Gal 5:17.

thing else than ordered affections. It is written of certain people that they were in great fear where there was no cause for fear;[2] they feared, that is, but inordinately. It was this that our Lord wanted to set in order in his disciples when he said: "I will show you whom you should fear,"[3] and David: "Come, children," he said, "listen to me; I will teach you the fear of the Lord."[4] He was also reproving men on the score of inordinate love who said: "I have come as a light into this world, and men loved darkness rather than light."[5] That is why the Bride says in the Song: "Set charity in order in me."[6] So, too, those were being cautioned about inordinate desire to whom it was said: "You do not know what you are asking;"[7] but were shown how to bring their crooked wills back to straight path when they heard: "Are you able to drink the cup that I am to drink? "[8] Again he taught them— at the time by word, but later by example also—how to set their will in order, when, at the beginning of his passion, praying that the cup might pass from him, he immediately added: "Nevertheless, not as I will; but as you will."[9] Thus we have received from God as part of our natural condition how to will, how to fear and how to love. In this we are creatures. But how to will the good, and how to fear God, and how to love God, we receive with grace's touch: in this we are creatures of God.

THE DIFFERENCE BETWEEN A GOOD AND A BAD FREE WILL

18. Created, then, to a certain extent, as our own in free-dom of will, we become God's as it were by good will. More-

2. See Ps 53:5 (Vg).
3. Lk 12:5.
4. Ps 34:11.
5. See Jn 3:19.
6. See Song 2:4 (Vg); and Bernard's "Apology to Abbot William," tr. Michael Casey, *The Works of Bernard of Clairvaux,* vol. 1, CF 1 (Spencer, Massachusetts, Cistercian Publications, 1970), p. 42, note 47. There is a whole subsection devoted to this ordering of charity, in P. Delfgaauw's study, "La Nature et les Degrés de l'Amour selon S. Bernard," *S. Bernard Théologien,* ASOC 9 (1953), 295-251. See also ibid., p. 274.
7. Mt 20:22.
8. Mt 20:22.
9. Mt 26:39.

over he makes the will good, who made it free; and makes it good to this end, that we may be a kind of first fruits of his creatures;[10] because it would have been better for us never to have existed than that we should remain always our own. For those who wished to belong to themselves, became indeed like gods, knowing good and evil; but then they were not merely their own, but the devil's.[11] Hence, free will makes us our own; bad will, the devil's; and good will, God's. This is the meaning of the words: "The Lord knows those who are his."[12] For to those who are not his he says: "Amen I say to you, I do not know you."[13] As long, therefore, as by bad will we belong to the devil, we are, in a certain sense, no longer God's; just as, when by good will we pass over to God, we cease to belong to the devil. "No one," in fact, "can serve two masters."[14] Furthermore, whether we belong to God or to the devil, this does not prevent us from being also our own. For on either side freedom of choice continues to operate, and so the ground of merit remains, inasmuch as, when we are bad we are rightly punished, since we have become so of our own free choice, or when we are good we are glorified, since we could not have become so without a similar decision of our will. It is our own will that enslaves us to the devil, not his power; whereas, God's grace subjects us to God, not our own will. Our will, created good (as must be granted) by the good God, shall nevertheless be perfect only when perfectly subjected to its Creator. This does not mean that we ascribe to it its own perfection, and to God, only its creation; since to be perfect is far more than to be made. The attributing to God of what is less excellent, and to ourselves of what is more, surely stands condemned in the very statement. Finally, the Apostle, feeling what he really was by nature and what he hoped to be by grace, said: "I can will what is right, but I cannot do it."[15] He realised that to will

10. See Jas 1:18.
11. See Gen 3:5.
12. 2 Tim 2:19.
13. Mt 25:12.
14. Mt 6:24.
15. Rom 7:18.

was possible to him as a result of free choice, but that for this will to be perfect he stood in need of grace. For, if to will what is evil is a defect of the willing faculty, then undoubtedly to will what is good marks a growth in this same faculty. To measure up to every good thing that we will, however, is its perfection.

19. In order, then, that our willing, derived from our free choice may be perfect, we need the twofold gift of grace: namely, true wisdom, which means the turning of the will to good, and full power, which means its confirmation in good.[16]

PERFECT GOOD WILL: A THREEFOLD GOOD

Now, perfect conversion is conversion to good, to the end that only fitting or permissible things may be found pleasing; and perfect confirmation in good is to the end that nothing of what is pleasing may any longer be found wanting. Then, in the end, shall the will be perfect, when it shall be fully whole and wholly full.[17] From the first moment of its existence, it possesses in itself a twofold goodness: the one, general, by the mere fact of creation, which means that anything created by a good God cannot be other than good (for "God saw everything he had made, and, behold, they were very good"[18]); the other, special, arising from its freedom of choice, by which it was made in the image of him who created it.[19] And if to these two goods we add a third, conversion

16. It is difficult to find a good rendering here. Since two key-terms are involved, it seems best to give Bernard's own sentence: "Ut ergo velle nostrum, quod ex libero arbitrio habemus, perfectum habeamus, duplici gratiae munere indigemus, et vero videlicet sapere, quod est voluntatis ad bonum conversio, et pleno etiam posse, quod est eiusdem in bono confirmatio." According to W. Williams, *The Treatise*, p. 33, note 1, whose translation I have adopted, "these (*vero sapere pleno posse*) would appear to be two of the gifts of the Holy Ghost, *sapientia* and *fortitudo*."

17. Again, it is not easy to do justice to Bernard's clever juggling: " . . . cum plene fuerit bona, et bene plena." W. Williams, *The Treatise*, p. 33, note 2, comments: "The 'plene bona' refers to *conversio*, and the 'bene plena' to *confirmatio*, which together effect the perfection of the will in the moral as distinct from the natural sphere."

18. Gen 1:31.

19. See Gen 1:26.

to the Creator, then it may rightly be regarded as perfectly good: good, that is, as part of a good creation; better within its own sphere of action; best in its being established in order. This latter implies the total conversion of the will to God, and its wholehearted, voluntary and devoted subjection. To such perfection of righteousness is due, and, in fact, is joined, the fullness of glory, because these two are so closely inter-related that neither can there be perfection of righteousness apart from fullness of glory, nor fullness of glory without perfect righteousness. In fine, righteousness of this kind can-not exist outside of glory, since glory can only be predicated of such righteousness. Wherefore it is well stated: "Blessed are those who hunger and thirst for righteousness, for they shall be satisfied."[20]

20. These are the two qualities mentioned above, true wis-dom, namely, and full power; wisdom referring to righteous-ness, and power to glory. But the terms "true" and "full" are added, the one in order to distinguish it from the wisdom of the flesh, which is death,[21] and from the wisdom of the world, which is folly with God,[22] and by which men are wise after their own fashion; (wise, that is, in performing evil[23]); and the other, to distinguish it from the power of those of whom it is said: "The powerful shall be powerfully tor-mented."[24] For neither true wisdom nor full power is to be found except when those two freedoms mentioned earlier, (namely, freedom of counsel and freedom of pleasure), form a combination with free choice. Now, I would regard as truly wise and fully powerful only the man who not merely is able to will a thing from his free choice,[25] but is able also, by

20. Mt 5:6.

21. See Rom 8:6 (Vg, followed by Bernard, uses *sapientia carnis* in Rom 8:7, and *prudentia carnis* in 8:6. The Greek has *phronema tes sarkos* in both cases, meaning "the general bent of thought, the practical tendency and effort of the Flesh" (Boylan, *St Paul's Epistle to the Romans*, [Dublin: Gill and Son, 1947], p. 134).

22. See 1 Cor 3:19.

23. See Jer 4:22.

24. See Wis 6:6 (Vg). The play is on the verb *posse* used above in contrast to *sapere* (see note 84); whence, *potentes potentor tormenta patientur* (Wis 6:6).

25. See Rom 7:18.

virtue of the remaining two, to do it. He would in this case be neither capable of willing what is evil, nor of lacking what he willed; the former, resulting from freedom of counsel, being true wisdom; the latter, from freedom of pleasure, full power. But what man is of such quality and so great that he can glory in this? [26] Or where, or when may it be obtained? Is it in this age? Indeed, did such a one live, he would be better than Paul, who openly confessed: "I cannot do it."[27] Can it be said of Adam in paradise? If it could, he would never have suffered exile from paradise.

26. See 1 Cor: 3:21.
27. See Rom 7:18.

CHAPTER SEVEN

WHETHER ADAM IN PARADISE WAS ENDOWED WITH THIS THREEFOLD FREEDOM HOW FAR HIS ENDOWMENT WAS LOST BY SIN

THE TIME HAS COME to examine what we put off doing earlier: whether the first human beings in paradise possessed all three of the freedoms referred to, freedom of choice, of counsel and of pleasure, or, in other words, freedom from necessity, from sin and from sorrow, or whether they had only two, or even only one of them. With regard to the first, there is no difficulty, when we recall how the argument already advanced has shown it clearly to exist in the just and sinners alike. Concerning the remaining two, it may fairly be asked whether Adam possessed them, either both or even one. Because, if he had neither, what did he lose? He certainly retained his freedom of choice, unharmed by the fact of his sin. If, then, he lost nothing, what difference did it make to him being expelled from paradise? But if he possessed any one of them, how did he lost it? For it is beyond doubt that, from the mere fact of sinning, he was, in the body, neither free from sin nor from sorrow. Besides, either of them once received, it could never be lost. Otherwise, neither his wisdom nor his power could be shown to have been perfect in the way defined above, as long as he could will what he ought not to will, and receive what he did not want to receive. Or is it that he had them in a certain measure, but could lose them because he did not possess them fully?

FREEDOM OF COUNSEL AND FREEDOM OF
PLEASURE, EACH HAS TWO DEGREES

The fact is that each of them admits of two degrees, a
higher and a lower. The higher freedom of counsel consists in
not being able to sin, the lower in being able not to sin.[1]
Again, the higher freedom of pleasure lies in not being able to
be disturbed, the lower in being able not to be disturbed.[2]
Thus, man received in his very nature, along with full freedom of choice, the lower degree of each of these freedoms;
and when he sinned, fell from both. In losing completely his
freedom of counsel, he fell from being able not to sin to not
being able not to sin. Likewise, from being able not to be
disturbed, he fell to not being able not to be disturbed, with
the total loss of his freedom of pleasure. There only remained, for his punishment, the freedom of choice through
which he had lost the others; that he could not lost. Enslaved
by his own will to sin,[3] he deservedly forfeited freedom of
counsel. Through his sin he became a debtor of death,[4] so
how could he hold on to his freedom of pleasure?

22. Three freedoms he had received. By abusing the one
called freedom of choice, he deprived himself of the others.
He abused it, in that what he had received for his glory, he
turned to his shame, in accordance with the words of Scripture: "Man, when he was in honor, did not understand; he
became like the senseless beasts."[5] Among all living beings,
to man alone was given the ability to sin, as part of his
prerogative of free choice. But he was given it, not that he
might, but rather that he might appear the more glorious did
he not sin when he was capable of doing so. What, in fact,
could afford him greater glory than that Scripture's words be
spoken of him, where it says: "Who is he, and we shall praise
him?"[6] But why such praise? "For he has done wonderful

---

1. See Augustine, *Of Correction and Grace* 12:33, for the same distinction.
2. Or, "to be upset," "made sorrowful."
3. See Rom 6:17f.
4. See Rom 5:12.
5. Ps 49:12 (Vg).
6. Sir 31:9f (Vg).

things in his life."[7] What kind of things? "He had the power to transgress," it says, "and he did not transgress, and to do evil and did not do it."[8] This honor he kept as long as he was sinless; but once he sinned, he lost it. He sinned, because he was free to sin, and free from no other source than his own freedom of choice, which bore within it the possibility of sinning. No failure this of the bestower, but rather of the abuser, who made over to the service of sin that faculty he had received for the glory of not sinning. For, though the root of his sin lay in the ability received, yet he sinned, not because he was able to, but because he willed to. So it was that, when the devil and his angels rebelled, others of their company refused to do so: not because they could not, but because they would not.

23. The sinner's fall, therefore, was not due to the gift of being able to, but to the vice of willing to. However, if he fell by the power of his will, this does not mean that he was equally free to rise again by that same power. The ability to remain standing lest he fall[9] was indeed given to his will, but not to get up again once he fell. It is not as easy to climb out of a pit as to fall into one. By his will alone, man fell into the pit of sin; but he cannot climb out of his will alone, since now, even if he wishes he cannot not sin.

---

7. Ibid.
8. Ibid.
9. See 1 Cor 10:12.

CHAPTER EIGHT

FREE CHOICE REMAINS AFTER SIN HAS TAKEN OVER

DOES THE FACT that he cannot not sin, then, put an end to free choice? No; but he lost free counsel by which previously he had enjoyed the ability not to sin. In the same way, the poor wretch may attribute his not being able any longer not to be disturbed to the fact that he has also lost freedom of pleasure by means of which previously he was able not to be disturbed.

ALTHOUGH MAN CANNOT SIN, NEVERTHELESS HE HAS NOT LOST FREE CHOICE

Free choice, consequently, still remains, even after man's sin, tinged with sorrow but intact. And the fact that he can in no way extricate himself either from sin or sorrow signifies, not the destruction of free choice, but the privation of the other two freedoms. For it does not belong to free choice, in itself, nor did it ever belong to it, to possess either power or wisdom, but only to will; nor can it make a creature wise or able, but only willing. He cannot therefore be considered as having lost free choice, if he has ceased to be wise or able, but only if he has ceased to be willing. For where there is no will, neither is there freedom. I am not saying that once a person ceases to will the good, but once he ceases simply to will—where it is not merely a question of the good ceasing in the will, but of the will itself ceasing in its entirety—must free choice also be said unquestionably to vanish. If he finds himself unable simply to will the good, this is a sign that he lacks

free counsel, not free choice. And if he finds himself powerless, not indeed to will the good, but to accomplish that good
which he already wills, let him recognise that it is not free
choice that is wanting to him, but free pleasure. Hence, if
free choice so follows the will everywhere that unless the will
ceases to function free choice will continue to operate, then
the will remains present equally in evil and in good; and free
choice likewise in evil and in good. And, as the will, even in a
state of sorrow, does not cease for all that to be the will, but
is called, and is in fact, a sorrowful will, (as it is also called,
and is, a happy will), so neither can any adversity or necessity
either destroy, or, in what concerns its own nature, in any
way diminish, freedom of choice.

25. But though it always carries on unimpaired, it cannot
of itself rise from evil to good as easily as it could of itself fall
from good to evil. And what wonder is it if it is unable to rise
of itself from its fallen condition, when in its standing it was
quite powerless to advance on its own to something better?
In a word, while to some extent it still enjoyed those other
two freedoms, it could not ascend from these lower degrees
to the higher, that is, from a state of being able not to sin and
being able not to be disturbed to that of not being able to sin
and not being able to be disturbed. Now, if with the help,
even in some small measure, of those freedoms, it was yet
unable to raise itself from the good to the better, how much
less chance does it stand, now that it is deprived of them, of
raising itself up by its own power from evil to that former
level which was good.

26. And this is where Christ comes in. In him, man possesses the necessary "power of God and the wisdom of
God,"[1] who, inasmuch as he is wisdom, pours back into man
true wisdom, and so restores to him his free counsel; and,
inasmuch as he is power, renews his full power, and so restores to him his free pleasure. As a result, being by the
former perfectly good, he may now no longer know sin; and
being, by the latter, completely happy, may no longer feel its

1. 1 Cor 1:24.

sting. Such perfection, nevertheless, must be awaited in the next life, when both these freedoms, at present lost, will be fully restored to free choice, not as it is given to any just man here on earth however perfect, and not as it was given even to the first human beings to enjoy them in paradise, but as the angels possess them now in heaven. Meanwhile, in "this body of death"[2] and in "the present evil age,"[3] we must be content simply with not giving way to sin from any concupiscence, and this we may do through our freedom of counsel; and with fearing no adversity for the sake of righteousness, and this we may do through our freedom of pleasure. In this sinful flesh,[4] however, and in this evil of the day,[5] it is no small wisdom not to consent to sin, though one cannot be rid of it altogether; and it is no inconsiderable power, manfully to despise adversity for the sake of truth, though one cannot yet, in happiness, avoid feeling it at times.

27. Here below, we must learn from our freedom of counsel not to abuse free choice, in order that one day we may be able fully to enjoy freedom of pleasure. Thus we are repairing the image of God in us, and the way is being paved, by grace, for the retrieving of that former honor which we forfeited by sin. Happy then will be the man who shall deserve to hear said of him: "Who is he, and we shall praise him? For he has done wonderful things in his life: who had the power to transgress, and did not transgress; to do evil and did not do it."[6]

---

2. See Rom 7:24.
3. Gal 1:4.
4. See Rom 8:3.

5. See Mt 6:34.
6. Sir 31:9f.

CHAPTER NINE

THE IMAGE AND LIKENESS OF THE CREATOR
CONSIST IN THIS THREEFOLD FREEDOM

I BELIEVE THAT in these three freedoms there is con-
contained the image and likeness of the Creator in which
we were made;[1] that in freedom of choice lies the image,
and in the other two is contained a certain twofold likeness.
Maybe, therefore, the reason why free choice alone suffers no
lessening or falling away, is that in it, more than in the
others, there seems to be imprinted some substantial image of
the eternal and immutable deity.

FREE CHOICE IS LIKE ETERNITY

For, although it had a beginning, it knows no end, nor has
it experience either of increase through righteousness or
glory, nor decrease through sin or sorrow. What could be
more like eternity without actually being eternity? Now, in
the other two freedoms, liable not only to partial diminution
but even to total loss, one sees, added to the image, a certain
more accidental likeness of the divine power and wisdom. By
a fault we lost them; by grace, we recovered them; and daily,
each in varying degrees, either advance in them or fall away.
They may be even irreparably lost; but also securely possessed, beyond the bounds of diminution.

29. Man was set in paradise, not indeed in the highest grade
of this twofold likeness to the wisdom and power of God,
but in a state quite close to it. For what could be closer to

1. See Gen 1:26.

not being able to sin or to be disturbed—in which condition, undoubtedly, the holy angels now live and God has lived always—than being able not to sin and not to be disturbed, in which state man was created? From this he fell away through sin and we along with him and in him only, through grace, to regain of it, not indeed the fullness, but some lower grade instead. True, we cannot be completely without sin or sorrow here on earth but we can, with the help of grace, avoid being overcome either by sin or by sorrow. Nevertheless, though Scripture says: "No one born of God commits sin,"[2] this refers to those only who are predestined to life: not that they never sin, but that sin is not imputed to them either because it is atoned for by due penance, or is covered up by charity. "Charity," as we know, "covers a multitude of sins,"[3] and: "Blessed is he whose transgression is forgiven, whose sin is covered," and: "Blessed is the man to whom the Lord imputes no guilt."[4]

BERNARD BEAUTIFULLY DISCERNS THE GRADES OF RATIONAL CREATURES

The highest angels, therefore, possess the highest grade of divine likeness, we the lowest; Adam enjoyed a degree somewhere in between, but the devils none whatever. For to the heavenly spirits it was given to persevere untouched by sin and sorrow; to Adam, to be without them admittedly, but not to persevere; and to us, not even to be without them, but only to be able not to yield to them. As the devil and his members, moreover, never will to resist sin, so neither are they ever able to escape its punishment.

FREE COUNSEL AND FREE PLEASURE DENOTE GOD'S LIKENESS AND FREE CHOICE HIS IMAGE

30. Both these freedoms (of counsel and of pleasure) by means of which true wisdom and power is communicated to

2. 1 Jn 3:9.
3. 1 Pet 4:8.
4. Ps 32:1f.

the rational creature God has dispensed according to his will and according to the way they were to vary in relation to causes, places, and times, inasmuch as they were possessed in slight measure on earth, more generously in paradise, fully in heaven, and not at all in hell. Freedom of choice, on the other hand, was never to change from the state in which it was created, but was always, considered in its own nature, equally present, whether in heaven or on earth or in hell. So it is that the other two freedoms correspond to God's likeness, but freedom of choice to his image. And, in fact, there is Scriptural testimony to show that, in hell, both those freedoms disappear, the ones, namely, which are said to pertain to his likeness. True wisdom (which, as we saw, is connected with freedom of counsel) disappears, as is clearly testified where we read: "Whatever your hand finds to do, do it with your might; for there is no work or thought or knowledge or wisdom in hell, to which you are going."[5] And of power, which is bestowed with freedom of pleasure, the Gospel says: "Bind him hand and foot, and cast him into the outer darkness."[6] What else does this binding of hand and foot mean than the utter privation of power?

EVIL WILL JUSTLY CONTINUES IN HELL, REBELLING AGAINST ITS PUNISHMENT

31. But someone may say: "How can it be that there is no element of wisdom there, when the ills which have to be borne must surely force one to repent of the evil conduct of the past? Can anyone not repent amid such sufferings? Or, on the other hand, can repentance for evil behavior possibly not include an alloy of wisdom? " This would certainly be a valid objection, if the sinful act alone were punished, and not the bad will. No one doubts the impossibility in those torments of finding pleasure in the repetition of the sinful act. Nevertheless, if the will remains evil even in hell's anguish,

5. Eccles 9:10.
6. Mt 22:13.

what weight can the denial of the act carry? Or how can anyone regard it as wise, merely because it has no inclination to indulge itself amid the flames? In fine, "Wisdom will not enter an ill-willed soul."[7] But how are we to prove that ill-will continues even in such sufferings? Well, to mention nothing else, they (the damned) are quite unwilling to be punished. Now, it is only right that people who have done things deserving of punishment should be punished. This means that they do not will what is right. And the more discordant it is with righteousness, the more is the will unrighteous, and consequently evil. There are two things which indicate an unrighteous will: delight in sinning and in having sinned without paying the penalty. What trace of true wisdom or of good will is to be found in such as take pleasure in sinning as long as it lies in their power, and when they are no longer able to, want nothing more than that their guilty past be left unavenged? But granted, for argument's sake, that they are sorry for having sinned, would they not still prefer to sin again had they the option, rather than to undergo sin's punishment? Yet, the former is wicked; the latter, righteous. When did a good will ever choose more what was wrong than what was right? Besides, those are not really sorry who do not grieve as much over the fact of having lived selfishly as over not being able to continue so doing. One last point: from the outside one can recognize the inside. As long as the body goes on burning in hellfire, so long is it evident that the will is fixed in malice. Accordingly, of the likeness contained in the freedoms of counsel and of pleasure, nothing remains or can remain in hell. But the image remains, even there, in free choice, permanent and unchanged.

7. Wis 1:4.

CHAPTER TEN

THROUGH CHRIST THE LIKENESS WHICH PROPERLY BELONGS
TO THE DIVINE IMAGE IS RESTORED IN US

NOT EVEN IN THIS PRESENT WORLD could the proper likeness be found, however, even the image would still have lain stained and deformed, had not that woman of the Gospel lit her lamp[1] (had Wisdom not appeared in the flesh, in other words), swept the house (of the vices), searched carefully for her lost coin (her image) which, its original luster gone, coated over with the skin of transgression, lay buried as it were in the dust; having found it, had she not not wiped it clean and taken it away from the "region of un-likeness;"[2] then, refashioned in its erstwhile beauty, made it like the saints in glory;[3] were she not, indeed, some day to make it quite conformable to herself—on that day, namely, when the words of Scripture would be fulfilled: "We know that when he appears we shall be like him, for we shall see him as he is."[4] To whom, in fact, could this work be better suited than to the Son of God, who, being the splendor and the figure of the Father's substance,[5] upholding all things by his word, was well qualified for it, from both these standpoints. So he was able to reform what was deformed, strengthen what was weak, and, dispelling with the godhead's splendor the shadows of sin, to make man wise, and, by the might of his word, to lend him strength against the tyranny of the demons.

1. See Lk 15:8.
2. See E. Gilson, op. cit., p. 45f.
3. See Sir 45:2 (Vg).

4. 1 Jn 3:2.
5. See Heb 1:3 (Vg).

33. That very form came,[6] therefore, to which free choice was to be conformed, because in order that it might regain its original form, it had to be reformed from that out of which it had been formed. Now, wisdom is the form and conformation means that the image fulfills in the body what form does in the world. Form "reaches mightily from one end to the other, and orders all things gently."[7] From end to end it reaches: that is, from the end of the heavens to the lower parts of the earth,[8] from the highest angel to the smallest worm. It reaches mightily, not indeed by moving about or filling up places, nor by mere official administration of its subject creature, but by a certain substantial and omnipresent strength, with which, undoubtedly, it powerfully moves, orders and administers all things. It is not forced to do this by any inner compulsion. Nor does it labor in its activity under the strain, but with tranquil intent orders all things gently. Again, it reaches from end to end: that is, from creation's birth to the end appointed by its Creator. This may be either the end to which nature impels it, or that which the cause speeds along, or that which grace concedes.[9] And it reaches mightily, since none of these is reached without its having been preordained by a most powerful providence in accordance with its will.[10]

34. This is the way, then, in which free choice should try to govern its body, as wisdom does the world, reaching mightily from end to end, or in other words so strongly commanding each sense and each member that it will not suffer sin to reign in its mortal body,[11] nor give its members over as instruments of wickedness,[12] but rather as slaves of righteous-

---

6. *Forma*: see Phil 2:6 (Vg). Cf. chapter 14 below, in which the same idea and terminology recur.
7. Wis 8:1 (Vg).
8. See Ps 19:6; Eph 4:9.
9. "This passage is a little obscure," remarks W. Williams.
10. See 1 Cor 12:11.
11. See Rom 6:12.
12. See Rom 6:13.

ness.[13] And so, man will no longer be the slave of sin, since he does not commit sin.[14] Further, set free from sin, he can now begin to recover his freedom of counsel and vindicate his dignity, while setting up in himself a worthy likeness to the divine image, restoring, in fact, completely his former loveliness. But let him take care to do this no less gently than mightily, that is, not reluctantly or under compulsion[15]—for this is the beginning, not the fullness of wisdom—but with prompt and ready will, which makes the offering acceptable, since "God loves a cheerful giver."[16] In this way, in all he does, he will be imitating wisdom, mightily resisting vices and gently at rest within his conscience.

35. We cannot achieve these things, however, without the help of him by whose example we are spurred on to desire them. With it, and by it, we ourselves are conformed, and transformed into the same image from glory to glory, as by the Spirit of the Lord.[17] But if by the Spirit of the Lord, then hardly by free choice. Let no one imagine therefore that free choice is so called because it concerns itself with good and evil with equal power or facility. It was indeed able to fall of itself; but could rise up again only through the Spirit of the Lord. Otherwise, neither God nor the holy angels, (since they are so good that they cannot be also evil), nor the fallen angels (since they are so bad that they are no longer capable of being good) could be said to have freedom of choice. Not only that; but we, too, would lose it after the resurrection, when we shall be inseparably united, some with the good and others with the bad.

NEITHER GOD NOR THE DEVIL LACKS FREE CHOICE

Now neither God nor the devil lacks free choice, since the fact that the former cannot be evil is not due to shaky neces-

13. See Rom 6:18.
14. See Jn 8:34 and Rom 6:6.
15. See 2 Cor 9:7.
16. 2 Cor 9:7; cf. Prov 22:8 (LXX).
17. See 2 Cor 3:18 (Vg).

sity but to a steady willingness in good and a willing steadiness while the later's being unable to seek after the good is not due to any violent oppression from outside but his own obstinate willingness in evil and his willing obstinacy. Free choice, consequently, is so called because whether in good or in evil, it makes the will equally free, since no one should be or can be referred to as either good or bad unless he is a willing subject. That is why he may rightly be said to be equally open to good and to evil, because on either side he feels an equal freedom in willing though not an equal ease in choosing.

CHAPTER ELEVEN

NEITHER GRACE NOR TEMPTATION DETRACTS
FROM FREEDOM OF CHOICE

THE CREATOR ENDOWED his rational creature, as we have said, with this prerogative of his divine dignity: that even as he himself was independent and master of his own will and hence not good by any necessity, so the creature, too, was made his own master to that extent that he would become evil only by his will and so justly be damned, or remain good by his will and deservedly be saved. Not that his will alone would be capable of gaining him salvation, but would never stand a chance of gaining it without his will. No one is unwillingly saved.

GOD JUDGES NO ONE WORTHY OF SALVATION
UNLESS HE FINDS HIM WANTING IT

For, what we read in the Gospel: "No one can come to me unless my Father draws him,"[1] and again elsewhere: "Compel people to come in,"[2] does not mean that, because the kindly Father who wills that all men be saved[3] appears as drawing and compelling many to salvation, this stands in the way of his judging worthy of salvation only such as he has previously proved to will it. Again, in frightening and in smiting men, his aim is not to save the unwilling, but rather to make them willing. In this way, changing their will from bad

1. See Jn 6:44.
2. Lk 14:23.
3. 1 Tim 2:4.

to good, he does not take away their freedom, but transfers its allegiance. Nevertheless, we have not always to be dragged along unwillingly; the blind or the weary seldom grumble at being helped along. Paul did not when he was lead by the hand to Damascus.[4] And that soul also willed to be drawn spiritually, who pleaded so earnestly for this in the Song of Songs: "Draw me after you," she said, "we will run in the odor of your ointments."[5]

37. The following texts, on the contrary all may be thought to force the will and undermine freedom: "Each person is tempted when he is lured and enticed by his own desire,"[6] and "A perishable body weighs down the soul, and this earthly tent burdens the thoughtful mind;"[7] and again those words of the Apostle: "I find in my members another law at war with the law of my mind and making me captive to the law of sin which dwells in my members."[8] Nevertheless, however much one may be assailed by temptation whether from within or from without, in regard to choice the will remains always itself and freely determines its own consent. With regard, on the other hand, to counsel and pleasure, it feels itself less free indeed, since the concupiscence of the flesh and the misery of life keep resisting; but it does not feel positively bad as long as it does not consent to the bad.

THE WORDS OF THE APOSTLE COMPLAINING HE IS MADE A CAPTIVE OF SIN

Finally, Paul, who complains of being made captive to the law of sin—doubtless because he has not full freedom of counsel—yet glories in the health of his consent to good, seeing that in this he is still in large measure free: "It is no longer I," he says, "that do it."[9] What makes you so sure of that, Paul? Because, he says, "I agree that the law of God is good,"[10] and "I delight in the law of God, in my inmost self."[11] If only the eye is simple, then he presumes the whole

4. See Acts 9:8.
5. Song 1:4 (Vg).
6. Jas 1:14.
7. Wis 9:15.

8. Rom 7:23.
9. Rom 720.
10. Rom 7:16.
11. Rom 7:22.

body to be full of light.[12] The consent of his will being unimpaired, he does not hesitate to profess that, although drawn to sin and captive to sorrow, he is still free in well-doing. In this confidence it is that he draws the general conclusion: "There is therefore no condemnation for those who are in Christ Jesus."[13]

12. See Mt 6:22.
13. Rom 8:1.

CHAPTER TWELVE

WHETHER ONE WHO, FOR FEAR OF DEATH OR PUNISHMENT, DENIES THE FAITH, IS TO BE EXCUSED FROM BLAME, OR TO BE REGARDED AS DEPRIVED OF FREE CHOICE

BUT NOW LET US CONSIDER for a moment those who are forced, whether by the fear of death or of some penalty, to deny their faith, though in word only, and see whether, according to this statement, there was either no guilt (in that their denial was purely verbal) or else that the will itself could be forced into a state of guilt (so that a person could will what obviously he did not will and free choice would perish). Since this latter is impossible—namely, that a man should simultaneously will and not will the same thing—our question is: how is it that evil can be imputed to those who in no way will the evil? This case is not identical with that of original sin, where someone not yet baptised is constrained on other grounds, not only unwillingly but even, for the most part, unwittingly. The Apostle Peter may serve as an example. He appears to have denied the truth against his own will: it was a matter of deny or die.[1] Fearing death, he denied. He did not wish to deny, but still less did he wish to die. Thus, unwillingly sure enough, he denied, for fear of death. Now, though the man was compelled to say with his tongue, and not with his will, what he did not want to say, he did not nevertheless, will other than what he was accustomed to will. His tongue was moved against his will. But what of the will? Was that changed? What did he actually want? Undoubtedly, to be what he was, Christ's disciple. And what did he say? "I do not know the man."[2] Why did he say

1. See Mt 26:70.   2. Mt 26:72.

this? He wanted to escape death. What was wrong with that?

THE WILL OF PETER WAS CULPABLE BECAUSE IT
CHOSE TO LIE RATHER THAN TO DIE

Here we have, therefore, two wills of the Apostle: the one, quite innocent, by which he wished not to die; the other, most praiseworthy, by which he rejoiced in the fact of being a Christian. In what, then, was he to blame? Was it that he preferred to lie rather than to die? Indeed this will of his was reprehensible; it meant that he was more interested in saving his body's life than his soul's: "A lying mouth destroys the soul."[3] And so he sinned, not without the consent of his own will either, weak and vapid indeed, but nonetheless free. He sinned, not by hating or rejecting Christ, but by loving himself to excess. Nor did the fear of the moment force his will into this perverse self-love; it proved it to exist. Without doubt, he already was such a man as this, though without being aware of it, when he heard from him to whom no secret was veiled: "Before the cock crows, you will deny me three times."[4] That weakness of will, unmasked, though not caused, by sudden fear, brought it to light not to Christ but to Peter; for Christ already "knew what was in man."[5] Insofar, therefore, as he loved Christ, that will of his undeniably suffered violence to make it speak in spite of itself; but insofar as he loved himself, he freely consented to speak on his own behalf. Had he not loved Christ, his denial would not have been unwilling; but had he not loved himself even more, there would not have been any denial. We must consequently grant that the man was forced, if not to change, yet to dissemble his own will: forced, I say, not to recede from the love of God, but somewhat to yield to love of self.

39. But does this imply that all our earlier assertion regarding the freedom of the will was mistaken, since we have discovered that the will can be forced? Yes, if it could be forced by some cause other than itself. If, however, it was

3. Wis 1:11.   4. Mt 26:34.

itself that did the forcing, being at once subjected and subjecting, then, just when it seemed to lose its freedom, it actually received it. For it was the first to generate the force to which it subjected itself.

PETER WAS NOT COMPELLED BUT BY HIS OWN WILL, CONSENTED IN SO FAR AS HE FEARED DEATH

Now, the fact that the will did generate this force means that it arose out of the will. But, if it was out of the will, then it was not necessary but voluntary. And, if voluntary, free. He then who was forced into denial by his own will, was forced because he willed it: or rather, he was not forced, but consented, not to any pressure from outside, but to his own will, to that will by which he wanted at all costs to avoid death. How otherwise would a woman's voice have been sufficient to tempt a holy tongue into pronouncing unholy words, had not the will, mistress of the tongue, assented? Finally, when later he came to control this excessive self-love and to love Christ as he ought to with his whole heart and soul and strength,[6] no threats or punishments could induce his will, however slightly, to yield its tongue as an instrument to sin,[7] but rather, courageously responding to the truth, he said: "We must obey God rather than men."[8]

THE TWOFOLD FORCE AGAINST FREE WILL: ACTIVE AND PASSIVE

40. There is, in fact, a twofold compulsion, by which we are forced either to do or to suffer something against our own will. Passive compusion (for that is what the first is rightly called) can sometimes occur without the voluntary consent of the sufferer but active compulsion never can. Consequently, evil which is brought about in us or relative to us is not imputable to us as long as we are unwilling. On the other hand, what is done by us is now not without fault on the part of the will. We are prevailed upon to will something

5. Jn 2:25.   7. See Rom 6:13.
6. See Mk 12:30.   8. Acts 5:29.

that would not happen did we not will it. There is thus also a certain active compulsion though this is inexcusable when it is voluntary. A Christian (let us say) was forced into denying Christ, sorrowfully, doubtless, yet willingly. He willed excessively to escape the threatening sword, and it was this will presiding within him which opened his mouth, not the sword he saw in front of him. The sword showed the will to be what it was; it did not force it. The will, not the sword, therefore, pushed the will into its guilty decision. As to those others whose will was healthy, they could be killed, but never made to yield. That is what had been foretold of them: "They shall do to you whatever they please";[9] to their limbs, that is, not to their hearts. It is not you who shall do whatever they please, it is they who do it; you shall suffer it. They shall torture your members, but have no effect on your will. They shall do their worst upon your flesh, but there will be nothing they can do about your soul.[10] Though the sufferer's body be in the power of the tormentor, the will is free. Their ferocity shall soon reveal if it is weak. If it is not, they shall not force it to be. Its weakness is its own, its health not its own, but from the Spirit of the Lord. And it is made healthy when it is renewed.

41. Now, renewal comes when, as the Apostle teaches, "beholding the glory of God, it is transformed into the same image from glory to glory (that is, from strength to strength) as by the Spirit of the Lord."[11]

FREE WILL STANDS BETWEEN FLESH AND SPIRIT

Between these two: the divine Spirit and the fleshly appetite, what is called in man free choice, or, in other words,

9. See Mk 9:13 par. (Vg: " ... they did to him whatever they pleased.")

10. See Mt 10:28. For the passage, "That is what had been foretold of them ... but there will be nothing they can do about your soul," certain other versions have: "That is what was said of John: They did to him whatever they pleased. Was it what *he* pleased? So they did with the other martyrs not what the martyrs pleased, but what they themselves pleased. They did to them, I say, what they pleased, but to their members, not to their hearts. They tortured their members, but failed to change their will. They did their worst upon their flesh, but were unable to do anything about their soul."

11. 2 Cor 3:18. For parenthesis, see Ps 84:7.

human will, occupies as it were a middle position. Able to go in either direction, it is, as it were, on the sloping side of a fairly steep mountain. It is so weakened in its desires by the flesh that only with the Spirit constantly helping its infirmity through grace[12] is it capable of righteousness (which, to quote the Prophet, is like the mountains of God[13]), capable of ascending from strength to strength right up to the summit. Without that help, borne by the pull of its own weight, it would tumble headlong down the precipice, from vice to vice. This pull would come not only from the law of sin originally implanted in its members, but from the habit of worldliness long implanted in its affections. Scripture recalls this twofold load on the human will in one short verse, when it says: "A perishable body weighs down the soul, and this earthly tent burdens the thoughtful mind."[14] And even as these two ills of our mortality do not injure, but test, those who do not consent, so neither do they excuse, but rather condemn, those who do. Thus there can be no salvation nor damnation without the previous consent of the will, lest freedom of choice might appear to be in any respect predetermined.

12. See Rom 8:26.
13. See Ps 36:6.
14. Wis 9:15.

CHAPTER THIRTEEN

HUMAN MERITS ARE GOD'S GIFTS

CONSEQUENTLY, that which in the creature is called free choice, is either justly condemned, since it is not preordained to sin by any external influence, or else is mercifully saved, an end it is quite incapable of achieving on its own. In all of this, however, the reader should remember that the idea of original sin is not being considered. For the rest, free choice must not seek the reason for its condemnation anywhere outside of itself, since its own fault alone condemns it; nor within itself the merit of its salvation, since mercy alone is responsible for saving it. Vain indeed, would be its efforts to do good were grace not at hand to help it; they would not even be, had they received no stimulus. Moreover, as Scripture observes, man's senses and thoughts are prone to evil.[1] Accordingly, as has been said, his merits must be seen as coming not from himself, but as descending from above, from the Father of lights,[2] provided only that those merits by which eternal salvation is gained be truly reckoned among the good endowments and perfect gifts.

GOD DIVIDED HIS GIFTS INTO MERITS AND GIFTS

43. For when God, our King from of old,[3] worked salvation in the midst of the earth,[4] he divided the gifts which he

1. See Gen 8:21.
2. See Jas 1:17.
3. See Ps 74:12.
4. Ibid.

gave to men into merits and rewards,[5] in order that, on the one hand, our merits might be our own here and now by free possession, and, on the other, by a gracious promise, we might await their recompense as our due, in fact even long for it, in the life to come. Paul draws attention to both these aspects when he says: "The return you get is sanctification, and its end, eternal life."[6] And again he says: "We ourselves, who have the first fruits of the Spirit, groan inwardly as we wait for adoption as sons,"[7] calling "sanctification" the first fruits of the Spirit; that is, those virtues by which in our present condition we are sanctified by the Spirit, in order that we may deservedly attain to adoption. These same things are once more promised in the Gospel to such as renounce the world, when it says: "He will receive a hundredfold, and inherit eternal life."[8] Hence, salvation is from the Lord,[9] not from free choice. Indeed, he is both salvation and the way to salvation, who said: "I am the salvation of the people,"[10] and elsewhere: "I am the way."[11] He who was also salvation and life made himself the way, so that no human being might boast.[12] If, then, merits are the good things of the pilgrim's way even as salvation and life are of the homeland, and if David spoke truly when he said: "There is none that does

---

5. See Eph 4:8; cf. Ps 68:18.
6. Rom 6:22.
7. Rom 8:23.
8. Mt 19:29.
9. See Ps 3:8.
10. See Ps 35:3 (Vg. "I am your salvation.") Bernard, however, is not quoting this psalm, but the Introit of the Mass for the nineteenth Sunday after Pentecost in the old rite: "Salus populi ego sum, dicit Dominus. . . ." In *Recueil d'Etudes sur S. Bernard et ses Ecrits,* I, (Roma: Edizioni di Storia e Letteratura, 1962), p. 307, Jean Leclercq asks the surprising question: "Did Bernard read the Bible? " In other words, when he quotes does he quote directly from a memory nourished directly on Scripture, or perhaps indirectly only? He replies in a note to the effect that Bernard was familiar with the books of the New Testament from personal reading, but with the Old Testament—and notably certain parts of the Wisdom literature—often through the liturgy. Bernard quotes this Introit again in SC 15:8; CF 4:112.
11. Jn 14:6.
12. See 1 Cor 1:29.

good, except for one"[13]—that one, namely, of whom it is also said: "No one is good but God alone"[14]—then both our works and his rewards are undoubtedly God's gifts, and he who placed himself in our debt by his gifts constituted us by our works real deservers. To form a basis for such meriting he deigns to make use of the ministry of creatures, not that he stands in any need of it, but that through this or by its means he may benefit them.

THE THREEFOLD OPERATION OF GOD THROUGH CREATURES: NAMELY, WITHOUT THEIR CONSENT, AGAINST THEIR CONSENT AND WITH THEIR CONSENT

44. He, therefore, accomplishes the salvation of those whose names are in the book of life,[15] sometimes through the creature yet without it, sometimes through the creature but against it, and sometimes through the creature and with it. Many a saving thing is rendered to man, in fact, by means of an insensible or irrational creature, which, consequently, is said to happen without it, since, lacking an intellect, it cannot act consciously. God also performs many things as a help to the salvation of many, by means of wicked men or wicked angels; but, since these latter are unwilling means, such divine activity may be said to take place against them.[16] For lending God a helping hand out of a desire to inflict injury, they hurt themselves as much as this perverse intention as they profit others by their useful action. Then there are those through whom and with whom God works; such are the good angels and men who both do and will whatever God wills. For God truly communicates the work he carries out through them to those who consent in will to what they do in act. Hence Paul, in telling of the many good deeds God had wrought through

13. Ps 14:3. The Hebrew means (as RSV renders it): "There is none that does good, no, not one." But Bernard interprets the Vg.
14. Lk 18:19.
15. See Phil 4:3.
16. W. Williams refers to the cases of Pharaoh (Exod 9:16; Rom 9:17), of Balaam (Num 22:18; 24:13) and of the Chaldeans (Hab 1:6).

him, qualifies: "though it was not I, but the grace of God which is with me."[17] He might have said "through me," but, because that would have been too little, he preferred to say "with me," supposing himself to be not merely the minister of the work through its accomplishment, but in some way also the associate of the worker by his consent.

45. Let us see in respect to the threefold manner of God's working, as just stated, what the creature merits for its service. What, in fact, can an instrument merit, by means of which and without which something is effected? What else but wrath can that merit against which a thing is done? What but grace that with which it is done?

WHAT EACH CREATURE MERITS

In the first case, accordingly, no merits are won; in the next, only demerits; and in the last, true merits. For when something good or evil is done by means of animals, these merit neither weal or woe, since they have not the capacity to consent either way. Much less do the stones merit, since they lack even sense-perception. The devil, or a wicked man, on the other hand, rationally both alive and alert, earns something for his trouble; only punishment, however, for they dissent from the good. But Paul, who is wholeheartedly in his work of evangelizing, so as not to be acting as a mere mercenary,[18] and anyone who follows his example, may rest assured that there is laid up for them a crown of righteousness[19] because they obeyed by the consent of their will. With an eye to man's salvation, God makes use, then, of irrational and even insensible creatures, as a pack-animal or tool which, their work done, are put aside. He uses rational but malevolent creatures after the manner of a switch which, once em-

17. 1 Cor 15:10.
18. See 1 Cor 9:16f. What Bernard is saying is that Paul's apostolic labor is meritorious in that he does it not as a hired workman working for pay, and hence by contract obligation, but *volens*, willingly, gladly, and without undue concern for remuneration.
19. See 2 Tim 4:8.

ployed on his son, he throws into the fire as a useless twig.[20]
He uses angels and men of good will, as his allies and com-
rades-in-arms whom, at the hour of victory, he will most
amply reward. To quote Paul again, boldly referring to himself and his imitators: "We are God's fellow-workers."[21] God,
therefore, kindly gives man the credit, as often as he deigns
to perform some good act through him and with him. That is
why we presume to apply to ourselves the titles of "God's
fellow-workers," co-operators with the Holy Spirit, meriters
of the kingdom, in that we have become united with the
divine will by our own voluntary consent.

20. See Jn 15:6.
21. 1 Cor 3:9.

CHAPTER FOURTEEN

WHAT PART IS TO BE ASSIGNED TO GRACE, AND WHAT
TO FREE CHOICE IN THE WORK OF SALVATION

ARE WE TO SAY, then, that the entire function and the sole merit of free choice lie in its consent? Assuredly. Not that this consent, in which all merit consists, is its own doing, since we are unable even to think anything of ourselves;[1] which is less than to consent.

GOOD THOUGHT IS FROM GOD, CONSENT AND ACT
ALSO ARE FROM HIM BUT NOT WITHOUT US

These words are not mine but the Apostle's, who attributes to God and not to his own choosing power, everything susceptible of good: thinking, willing, and accomplishing for his good pleasure.[2] If, then, God works these three things in us, namely thinking, willing and accomplishing the good, the first he does without us; the second, with us; and the third, through us. By suggesting the good thought, he goes one first step ahead of us; by also bringing about the change of our ill will, he joins it to himself by its consent; and by supplying consent with faculty and ability, the operator within makes his appearance outwardly through the external work that we perform. Of ourselves, we cannot, of course, take that first step. But he who can find no one who is good, can save no one without himself first stepping into the lead. There can be

1. See 2 Cor 3:5.
2. See Phil 2:13.

no doubt, therefore, that the beginning of our salvation rests with God, and is enacted neither through us nor with us. The consent and the work, however, though not originating from us, nevertheless are not without us.

NEITHER CONSENT NOR THE ACT ARE ACCOMPLISHED WITHOUT GOOD WILL

So neither the first, since we are in no way involved in it; nor the last, which results, more often than not, from useless fear or damnable hypocrisy; but only the second, redounds to our merit. Good will suffices on its own at times; if it is wanting, everything else is of no avail. Of no avail to the agent, that is, but not to the beholder. Thus, intention is capable of merit; action of giving example; and the good thought preceding both, only of arousing from inertia.

47. We must therefore be careful, whenever we feel these things happening invisibly within us and with us, not to attribute them to our own will, which is weak; nor to any necessity on the part of God, for there is none; but to that grace alone of which he is full. This it is which arouses free choice, when it sows the seed of the good thought; which heals it, by changing its disposition; which strengthens it, so as to lead it to action; which saves it from experiencing a fall. It so co-operates with free choice, however, that only in the first case does it go a step ahead of it; in the others, it accompanies it. Indeed, its whole aim in taking the step ahead is that from then on it may co-operate with it. What was begun by grace alone, is completed by grace and free choice together, in such a way that they contribute to each new achievement not singly but jointly; not by turns, but simultaneously. It is not as if grace did one half of the work and free choice the other; but each does the whole work, according to its own peculiar contribution. Grace does the whole work, and so does free choice—with this one qualification: that whereas the whole is done *in* free choice, so is the whole done *of* grace.

48. We trust the reader may be pleased to find that we have never strayed far from the Apostle's meaning, and that wherever our words may wander, we find ourselves often return-

ing to almost his very words. For what else does what we are saying amount to but: "So it depends not upon man's will or exertion, but God's mercy? "[3] He does not say this as if it were possible for a person to will or to run in vain;[4] what he means is that the man who wills and runs would glory not in himself, but in him from whom he received in the first place the power both to will and to run. In a word: "What have you that you did not receive? "[5]

THE THREEFOLD OPERATION OF GOD: CREATION, FORMATION, CONSUMMATION

You are created, healed, saved. Which of these, O man, comes from you? Which is not impossible to free choice? You could neither create yourself, since you were not there to do so; nor, when in sin, could you restore yourself to grace; nor raise yourself from the dead, to say nothing of those other good things,[6] which are either necessary to those who have to be healed, or laid up in store for those who are to be saved. This is obvious enough in the case of creation and salvation. Yet, no one doubts it even in regard to justification except the man who, being ignorant of the righteousness that comes from God and seeking to establish his own, does not submit himself to God's righteousness.[7] For can it be that, while acknowledging the power of the Creator and the glory of the Savior, you are ignorant of the righteousness of the Healer? "Heal me," said the Prophet, "and I shall be healed; save me, and I shall be saved; for you are my praise."[8] He acknowledged the righteousness of God, and hoped at the same time both to be healed of his sin by him and to be cut free from sorrow. Hence he rightly declared that God, not himself, was his praise. For this reason also, David cried out: "Not to us, O Lord, not to us, but to your name give glory";[9] for it was from God that he was looking

3. Rom 9:16.
4. See Gal 2:2.
5. 1 Cor 4:7.
6. See 1 Cor 2:9.

7. See Rom 10:3.
8. Jer 17:14.
9. Ps 115:1.

for both robes, that is to say, the robe of righteousness and the robe of glory.[10]

THE SELF-RIGHTEOUS MAN DOES NOT KNOW THE RIGHTEOUSNESS OF GOD

Who is unaware of God's righteousness? The self-righteous man. And who is he? The man who imagines that his merits come from some source other than from grace. Further, it is the one who made what he would save who also provides the means of salvation. He, I mean, bestows the merits, who in the first place made those on whom he would bestow them. "What shall I give back to the Lord," he says, "for all that he has (he does not say *given* but) *given back* to me?"[11] He proclaims that being and righteousness alike he has from God, lest, were he to deny either, he might lose both: separating himself from the source of his righteousness and so condemning his being.[12] But now, in the third place, he finds that which in his turn he should repay: "I will take," he says, "the cup of salvation."[13] This cup of salvation is the Savior's blood. Hence, if you lack anything you can call your own, which you might give back even for the second gift of God to you, from what source do you promise yourself salvation? "I will call," he says, "on the name of the Lord,"[14] that name upon which, whoever calls shall be saved.[15]

49. Those, therefore, who are possessed of true wisdom, acknowledge a threefold operation, not indeed of free choice, but of divine grace in, or concerning, free choice. The first is creation; the second, reformation; and the third, consummation. Created first in Christ[16] unto freedom of will, by the

---

10. For the "robe of glory," see Sir 45:7 and 5:11. The "robe of righteousness" is possibly a reference to Is 61:10, Bar 5:2 or Eph 6:14. Otherwise it does not occur in the Vg.

11. Ps 116:12.

12. "His self-righteousness," explains W. Williams, "would deprive him of grace, and the loss of grace would mean the death of his soul."

13. Ps 116:13.

14. Ibid.

15. See Acts 2:21; 3:12.

16. See Eph 2:10.

second we are reformed through Christ unto the spirit of freedom,[17] lastly to reach fulfillment with Christ unto the state of eternity. It had to be, in fact, that what had no existence should be created by one who had; that what was deformed should be reformed through the Form; that the members should be perfected in no other way than with the head. This will happen when we all shall have attained "to mature manhood, to the measure of the stature of the fullness of Christ,"[18] when Christ who is our life, appearing, we also shall appear with him in glory.[19] Seeing, then, that fulfillment takes place in relation to us, or even in us, but not by us; whereas creation happens also without us; reformation alone, occuring as it does to some extent with us on account of our voluntary consent, will be reckoned for us as merit.

INTENTION–AFFECTION–MEMORY

These merits are our fasting, watchings, continence, works of mercy and other virtuous practices, by means of which, as is evident, our inner nature is renewed every day.[20] Our intention, bent down under the weight of earthly cares, rises again slowly from depths to heights; the affection, languishing in fleshly desires, gradually gains strength for spiritual love; and our memory, sullied by the shame of former deeds, but now become clean once more with continual good works, reaches each day a new measure of joy.[21] In these three things it is that interior renewal consists: rightness of intention, purity of affection, and the remembrance of good work, this last leading the memory, in full self-awareness, to shed its light about it.

17. See 2 Cor 3:17f.
18. Eph 4:13.
19. See Col 3:4.
20. See 2 Cor 4:16.
21. Though Bernard adopts Augustine's division of the soul into memory, reason, and will, he nevertheless understands "memory" in its commonly accepted sense of remembering faculty, and not as Augustine understood it. See E. von Ivanka's essay, "La Structure de l'Ame selon S. Bernard," *S. Bernard Théologien,* (above, note 13). Also Venuta, *Libero Arbitrio e Libertà della Grazia,* p. 44, note 1.

50. Since it is clearly the divine Spirit who activates these things in us, they are God's gifts; yet because they come about by the assent of our will, they are our merits. "For it is not you who speak," he says, "but the Spirit of your Father speaking through you."²² And the Apostle: "Do you desire proof that Christ is speaking in me? "²³ If Christ, then, or the Holy Spirit is speaking in Paul, is he not also at work in him? "For I will not venture to speak," he says, "of anything except what Christ has wrought through me."²⁴ But what does this mean? If, since the words and works of the one speaking or working through Paul are not Paul's but God's where are Paul's merits? And what becomes of those confident words of his: "I have fought the good fight, I have finished the race, I have kept the faith. Henceforth there is laid up for me the crown of righteousness, which the Lord, the righteous judge, will award to me on that Day"? ²⁵ Did he perhaps think that a crown would be laid up for him because these things were wrought through him? But then many good things happen by means of the wicked, whether they be angels or men, without their being reckoned for them as merits. Or was it not rather that they were done with his co-operation, that is, with his good will? "For," said he, "if I preach the gospel unwillingly, I am entrusted with a commission; but if I do it willingly it is to my glory."²⁶

51. There is another question: if not even so much as the will, on which all merit depends, is from Paul himself, how can he refer to the crown, which he presumes is laid up for him, as a crown of righteousness? Is it that one can justly demand as a debt whatever is promised gratis? ²⁷

22. Mt 10:20.
23. 2 Cor 13:3.
24. Rom 15:18.
25. 2 Tim 4:7f.
26. See 1 Cor 9:16f.
27. The answer, of course, is "yes." On the important and encouraging New Testament idea of God's "steadfastness" or "faithfulness" (*pistotes*), see 1 Cor 1:9; 10:13; 2 Cor 1:18; 1 Thess 5:24; 2 Thess 3:3; Heb 10:23; 11:11; 2 Tim 2:13; 1 Jn 1:9; 1 Pet 4:19.

THE CROWN PAUL EXPECTS IS THE CROWN OF GOD'S RIGHTEOUSNESS, NOT HIS OWN

He says: "I know in whom I have believed, and I am sure that he is able to guard what has been entrusted to me."[28] He calls the promise of God something that has been entrusted to him. Because he believed the one promising, with confidence he repeats the promise, which, arising out of mercy, must be fulfilled out of justice. Hence, the crown Paul awaits is a crown of righteousness, but of God's righteousness, not his own. It is only just that he should deliver what he owes; and he owes what he promised. This is the righteousness Paul is relying on, the promise of God, lest, in any way despising it, and seeking to establish his own, he might be failing to submit to God's righteousness.[29] God, however, wished to have him as partaker of his righteousness in order that he might also make him deserving of a crown. For he made him partaker of his righteousness and deserving of a crown when he deigned to choose him as his fellow-worker in the works to which the promise of the crown was attached. But he chose him as his fellow-worker when he made him a willing person, or, in other words, a consenter to his will. Thus, while the will is given in view of helping, the helping is reckoned as merit. If, therefore, the willing is from God, so too is the merit. Nor can it be doubted that it belongs to God "both to will and to work for his good pleasure."[30] God is, in consequence, the author of merit, who both applies the will to the work, and supplies the work to the will. Besides, if the merits which we refer to as ours are rightly so called, then they are seed-beds of hope, incentives to love, portents of a hidden predestination, harbingers of happiness, the road to the kingdom, not a motive for playing the king. In one word: it is those whom he made righteous, not those whom he found already righteous, that he has magnified.[31]

28. 2 Tim 1:12.
29. See Rom 10:3.
30. Phil 2:13.
31. See Rom 8:30.

SELECTED BIBLIOGRAPHY

ON GRACE AND FREE CHOICE

Critical Edition

"De gratia et libero arbitrio." Ed. J. Leclercq and H. M. Rochais. *S. Bernardi opera*. Vol. 3 (Rome: Editiones Cistercienses, 1963) pp. 165-203.

Charpentier, M. "Traité de la Grace et du Libre Arbitre" *Oeuvres complètes de Saint Bernard.* Vol. 2 (Paris: Vives, 1866) pp. 494-531.

Dies Ramos, G. "De la gracia y del libre arbitrio," *Obras completas de San Bernardo.* Vol. 2, Biblioteca de Autores Cristianos, 130 (Madrid: Editorial Catolico, 1955) pp. 931-974.

Williams, Watkin W. *The Treatise of St Bernard Concerning Grace and Free Will* (New York: Macmillan/ London: SPCK, 1920).

Studies

Bavaud, G. "Les rapports de la grâce et des libre arbitre. Un dialogue entre saint Bernard, saint Thomas d'Aquin et Calvin," *Verbum Caro,* 14 (1960) 328-338.

Châtillon, J. "Influence de saint Bernard sur le scolastique," *Saint Bernard Théologien: Actes du Congrès di Dijon, 15-19 septembre 1953.* ASOC 9 (1953) 268-288.

Danielou, J. "St Bernard et les pères grecs," Ibid., pp. 46-55.

Dimier, A. "Pour la fiche *spiritus libertatis,*" *Revue du moyen âge latin* 3 (1947) 56-60.

Faust, V. "Bernhards 'Liber de Gratia et Libero Arbitrio': Bedeutung, Quellen und Einfluss," *Analecta Monastica* 6. Studia Anselmiana, 50 (Rome, 1962), 35-52.

Forest, A. "Das Erlebnis des *Consensus Voluntatis* beim heiligen Bernhard," *Bernhard von Clairvaux, Mönch und Mystiker* (Wiesbaden 1955), pp. 120-127.

Gilson, E. *The Spirit of Medieval Philosophy* (New York, 1940).

Gilson, E. *The Mystical Theology of Saint Bernard* (New York, 1940).

Hiss, W. *Die Anthropologie Bernhards von Clairvaux* (Berlin, 1964).

Javelet, R. *Image et ressemblance au douzième siècle.* 2 vols. (Paris, 1967) 1:189-197.

Kleineidam, E. "De triplici libertate. Anselm von Laon oder Bernhard von Clairvaux? " *Cîteaux* 11 (1960) 56-62.

Lottin, O. "Libre arbitre et liberté depuis saint Anselme jusqu'à la fin du XIIIe siècle," *Psychologie et moral au XIIe et XIIIe siècles.* 6 vols. (Louvain Gembloux, Mont César, 1942-1960) 1:11-224.

Otto, S. *Die Funktion des Bildbegriffes in der Theologie des 12 Jahrhunderts.* Beiträge zur Geschichte der Philosophie und Theologie des Mittelalters 40:1 (Münster, 1963).

Sartori, L. "Natura e Grazia nella Dottrina di San Bernardo," *Studia Patavina,* 1 (1954) 41-64.

Schaffner, O. "Die 'nobilis Deo creatura' des heiligen Bernhard von Clairvaux," *Geist und Leben,* 23 (1950) 43-57.

Standaert, Maur. "La doctrine de l'image chez saint Bernard," *Ephemerides Theologicae Lovaniensis,* 23 (1947) 70-129. Also in *In Sylloge Excerptorum e Dissertationibus* 14-4 (Louvain, 1947).

——. "Le principe de l'ordination dans la théologie spirituelle de saint Bernard," *Collectanea OCR* 8 (1946) 178-216.

Venuta, G. *Libero Arbitrio e Libertà della Grazia nel Pensiero di S. Bernardo.* (Rome: Ferrari, 1953).

Von Ivánka, E. "La structure de l'âme selon saint Bernard." *Saint Bernard Théologien,* pp. 202-208.

INDEX

On Grace and Free Choice
(Numerals refer to paragraph numbers)

CISTERCIAN PUBLICATIONS

Titles Listing

1977

THE CISTERCIAN FATHERS SERIES

THE WORKS OF BERNARD OF CLAIRVAUX

THE WORKS OF WILLIAM OF ST THIERRY

THE WORKS OF AELRED OF RIEVAULX

THE WORKS OF GUERRIC OF IGNY

OTHER WRITERS

THE CISTERCIAN STUDIES SERIES

CISTERCIAN STUDIES

MONASTIC TEXTS AND STUDIES